Glitte[r in]
the Sun

A Bible Study Searching for
Truth in the Twilight Saga

Jane Wells

Read The Spirit Books

an imprint of
David Crumm Media, LLC
Canton, Michigan

For more information and further discussion, visit
http://www.GlitterInTheSun.com

Cover art and design by
Rick Nease
www.RickNeaseArt.com

All scripture references are King James Version

Published By
Read The Spirit Books
an imprint of
David Crumm Media, LLC
42015 Ford Rd., Suite 234
Canton, Michigan, USA

For information about customized editions, bulk purchases
or permissions, contact David Crumm Media, LLC at
info@DavidCrummMedia.com

Contents

Preface from the Editor

GLITTER IN THE SUN. I was intrigued by the title before I even read Jane Wells' manuscript or Stephenie Meyer's *Twilight* series. What a great description of people of faith! People who reflect the light of the eternal God *glitter in the sun*! Those familiar with the *Twilight* series know that the phrase refers to vampires, as they avoid sunlight so as not to "glitter in the sun" and reveal their true identity. Faith should be similarly as obvious. People of faith should radiate warmth and light. Your true identity is revealed as you reflect the light of God.

Jane Wells, in *Glitter in the Sun*, provides a Bible study based on the enormously popular *Twilight* series. Jane brings years of experience as a popular small group Bible study leader/teacher to this book. As you read, you are quickly aware that not only is Jane passionate about the *Twilight* series; she is even more enthusiastic about the Christian faith. Jane teaches her beliefs from the Bible and shares, frankly and candidly, her own faith story. She is open and sincere as she relates both tender and tough times. I'm sure readers will not only appreciate Jane's honesty and genuineness but also find inspiration. Her unique sense of humor flows throughout *Glitter in the Sun*.

Glitter in the Sun is written from Jane's evangelical, Pentecostal perspective. We each bring our own religious bias to our writing, to discussion and to study. Jane finds common ground with a book series written by a Mormon. She finds spiritual truths in these fictional stories. No matter where you are coming from, theologically, I think you can find common ground in this study.

There is much within this book for discussion. Small groups offer opportunities for growing deeper in faith, as participants listen and talk about their journeys and experiences. Pay attention to your own stories and perspectives.

In the Worksheets following each chapter, I offer suggestions for small group activities and questions for group discussions. The small group activities offer implicit paths to the subject; these tap into areas of the brain beyond the linear, into creative and intuitive aspects perhaps not readily apparent. Some may seem a bit trivial or frivolous, but these experiences help those who may not feel comfortable to open up and talk more freely. The exercises may even unlock feelings and experiences. They build relationships in non-threatening ways. Some include spiritual disciplines, including various ways to pray.

The questions for group discussion are meant to be discussion starters. If a specific question isn't working, move to the next. Don't feel you must answer them all. The questions are designed to provoke meaningful discussion and spiritual growth. You might spend an entire session on one question. You will also bring your own questions. Some of the chapters include a Going Deeper Bible Study from Jane, offering additional scriptures to consider. Adapt the study to fit your particular group's needs.

Discover for yourself ways to "glitter in the sun."

Blessings,
Beth Miller

A Couple Caveats to Start

GLITTER IN THE SUN is a small group Bible study based on the *Twilight* series. Obviously, participants who have read the *Twilight* series will have an advantage. On the other hand, if you've never read the *Twilight* saga, some aspects of the study might be lost on you.

Glitter in the Sun does not attempt to give background, character summaries or details from the *Twilight* books. *Glitter in the Sun* is a Bible study, plain and simple. This study uses a popular work of modern fiction as a conversation starter for small group Bible study and discussion aimed at spiritual growth. Other writers can provide analysis, critique and review of this series; however, that is not the intent of this study. Online summaries of the *Twilight* series can offer insight into plot and major themes.

The *Twilight* saga is fiction. Please take special note of this ...*fiction*. In the real world—the wake up, get out of bed and put your feet on the floor world—there is no such thing as a vampire. Vampirism is an unconventional fascination in some corners of our culture built on myths. Perhaps it is an attractive fantasy for those who feel distant from compassionate communities or alienated from the Church.

Vampires are the subject of legends and folklore. They are typically portrayed as former humans transformed into scary, terrifying evil beings that prey on others. In the *Twilight* series, Stephenie Meyer proposes the option of "good vampires" who choose to drink animal rather than human blood.

Perhaps the phenomenal success of the *Twilight* series is not the result of a keen interest in the vampire culture; rather, it might be a universal longing for love. I think this is the greatest appeal of the novels and why they leave the reader wanting more. There is obviously a universal truth at play: each of us is born with a longing to be eternally, unconditionally loved. Only God can offer this absolute, perfect love. What hinders us from experiencing God's irresistible, all-consuming love? Many Christian writers—including C.S. Lewis, whose novels also are hugely popular with young readers—identify this antagonist as the devil, or Satan. What forces thwart us from living in God's glorious, comprehensive love?

Thankfully, God's love is persistent. "Calling cards" to His grace are everywhere. In the Book of Job, it suggests that even rainstorms can be the means of slowing us down enough to pay attention to this God of love (Job 37:5-7). Made in God's image, we echo God's design. Thus the love story of Edward wooing Bella reverberates God's desire for our love and devotion. It also indicates our yearning for God's love and care.

Twilight Cheat Sheet

Main Characters

- Bella Swan: The lead character and narrator of the novels. Bella moved from Phoenix, Arizona to Forks, Washington in the middle of her junior year of high school.
- Charlie Swan: Bella's divorced and single father, who is the Chief of Police in the small town of Forks.
- Renee (Swan) Dwyer: Bella's recently remarried mother, who lived with Bella in Phoenix.

The Cullen Family

- Carlisle Cullen: The patriarch of a "vegetarian" family of vampires who works as a doctor to strengthen his resistance against the scent of human blood. The Cullens call themselves "vegetarian" as a sort of inside joke, because they refuse to feed on human blood and instead choose to live on animal blood. The Cullens' "vegetarian" lifestyle goes against the grain of their vampire nature and culture—and the expectations of other vampires in the world.
- Esme (Platt-Evinson) Cullen: Carlisle's wife. Immensely compassionate, she is the clan's mother figure.
- Edward (Masen) Cullen: Carlisle's first attempt at changing a human into a vampire. Perpetually 17, Edward is Bella's love interest. Although he has nearly 100 years of human blood abstinence under his belt, the scent of Bella's blood is particularly appealing to

him. The struggle between his love for Bella and his hunger for her blood is a recurring theme in the series.

- Rosalie Hale/Cullen: Carlisle found and changed the beautiful Rosalie after she was beaten, raped and left for dead. She is married to Emmett.
- Emmett (McCarty) Cullen: Built like the bear that nearly mauled him to death before his change to vampire, Emmett is unafraid of confrontation but typically laid-back in character.
- Alice (Mary Alice Brandon) Cullen: Alice does not remember her human life; only waking up alone as a vampire with the ability to see the future, which is how she found Jasper and then the Cullens.
- Jasper (Whitlock) Hale/Cullen: As a human, Jasper was a Major in the Confederate Army when an ambitious vampire named Maria changed him and put him in charge of her vampire army. Of all the Cullens, Jasper has the hardest time with the "vegetarian" lifestyle. Jasper is Alice's significant other.
- Renesmee Cullen: The half-human/half-vampire child and the result of human Bella and vampire Edward's honeymoon. Renesmee's name is a contraction of *Rene(e)* and *Esmee*, but quickly was shortened to *Nessie*— much to Bella's chagrin.

The Wolf pack

- Jacob Black: The son of the Quileute tribal chief, a werewolf and the third side of Bella's love triangle.
- Quil Ateara V: Jacob's friend, a Quileute tribal member and a fellow werewolf.
- Sam Uley: The Alpha of the werewolf pack; the first of his generation to experience the change from human to werewolf.

- Emily Young: Sam's fiancé and the woman Sam has imprinted on for life. Emily has three disfiguring scars on the right side of her face from a time when Sam was standing too close when he phased into his werewolf form and accidentally clawed her.

Books

- *Twilight*: As a junior in high school, Bella Swan moves from Phoenix to Forks, the rainiest town in Washington, where she meets the handsome and mysterious Edward. Edward turns out to be a vampire who has chosen to live on animal blood, although even with nearly a century of human blood abstinence under his belt, the scent of Bella's blood is all but irresistible to him. Not killing Bella the moment they meet takes all of Edward's 100 years of discipline. Even after he gets to know and love her, Edward struggles with the physical desire to kill Bella just to satisfy his appetites—even while he and the Cullens defend her from other vampires who merely see her as a meal.

- *New Moon*: Edward thinks Bella would be safer in a world without vampires, and he talks his family into moving away from Forks. In her heartbreak, Bella finds comfort in the company of an old friend and Quileute tribal member, Jacob. But when Jacob begins revealing his werewolf nature, Bella is left alone once again. When news of a cliff diving incident—the result of Bella's drastic attempts to dull the pain of her loneliness—gets to Edward, he thinks she is dead and attempts "suicide by Volturi." The Volturi, one of the oldest and largest vampire clans in the world, consider themselves enforcers of the vampire code and kill any vampire who reveals his nature to humans or breaks vampire law. Bella, with Alice's help, rushes to Italy (the home of the Volturi) to prevent Edward from stepping into the sunlight and "glittering in the sun," therefore revealing his vampire nature to humans and forcing the Volturi to kill him.

- *Eclipse*: The Cullens return to Forks in the third part of this series, as Edward discovered he couldn't live without Bella, either. Jacob is furious that Edward has returned and that Bella has taken him back—with personal feelings for Bella put aside, Jacob is compounded by the natural enmity between werewolves and vampires. However, when Bella's life is threatened, the Cullens join forces with the Quileute werewolves to save her life and prevent the slaughter of many innocent humans.

- *Breaking Dawn*: In the final book, Edward and Bella get married. A few months later, Bella nearly dies giving birth to their daughter: a vampire-human hybrid who grows at a phenomenal rate. Bella is only saved by being transformed into a vampire. Word gets out of the half-breed child, and the Volturi covet the child as well as the supernatural gifts the other Cullens use. The Cullens vow to fight to the death to protect one another and their way of life. Jacob, having imprinted on Renesmee as the love of his life, brings the entire werewolf pack to the epic battle.

Introduction
Major Jasper Whitlock, Ma'am

THE CULLEN FAMILY WAS an oddity among oddities: vampires who did not drink human blood. But it wasn't until Jasper told Bella his personal history that she realized just how different his background was from those of the rest of the family.

Jasper was a warrior, a Confederate soldier, before being changed into a vampire. After that he was the trusted captain of a ruthless vampire queen. For Jasper, human life had about the same value as livestock; he was guilty of destroying thousands of lives. He fought other vampires for dominance and killed those who outlived their usefulness to his master. Eventually, the ruthlessness of those crimes began to weigh on his conscience. He left the only life he knew—one of violence and self-gratification—to find another way. Finally, he found hope and peace when he stumbled upon Alice and became a member of the Cullen family.

What led Jasper to seek another way of life? What motivates you to change? Have you ever sensed circumstances nudging you in a different direction? Has it ever occurred to you that sometimes there might be intention behind them?

In many ways, I had it easy. From a time before I can remember, I knew both of my parents loved me and each other without reservation or qualification. I knew God loved me, too: I heard it every day from my parents and every week at church. That is not true for everyone. So when I turned away from God to "try out" what the world had to offer, I knew what I was missing. It did not take long to realize exactly Who I needed to seek; Who could fill the aching void.

I simply needed to go home. That is exactly what it felt like—going home to a family that had missed me madly and only wanted to heal my wounds and restore me to health. The God Who had created me, much like my own father and mother, held open the door the whole time.

What if I hadn't known how to get home? What if I had never experienced a family that longed for me? What if, like Jasper, I had no idea that any other way of life was possible? What would I have done with that hungry black hole? The thought makes me shudder.

Prevenient grace is a term I learned in church school that means "God stacks the deck in favor of you finding The Way." *Prevenient* literally means "anticipatory, something that goes before." Before you are even aware of it, the Spirit of God is at work in the world and through others to lead you home. God's desire is that all souls return to their creator, but He anticipates that you might need some help getting there. To that end God plants clues, hints and pictures of grace and love everywhere: the glory of a sunrise or sunset, the cool breeze on a hot day, the perfect timing of "coincidence" or the generosity and kindness of others. Even a novel that stirs up lurking emptiness and sends you seeking something more can become a "means of prevenient grace." Maybe *prevenient grace* brought this book into your hands at this particular point in time. The question is: What are you going to do about it?

Like the Cullen men, God is a complete gentleman. While He will hold open doors for you, God will not force you through. Love never forces its way. Free will results from perfect love. It gives you a choice. So God waits while you decide how to answer the gentle question: "Will you come home to Me?"

CHAPTER 1

Welcome to Forks

BELLA DECIDES TO MOVE to Forks, Washington from Phoenix, Arizona to please her parents. However, she is not particularly happy with the consequences of that choice. She misses her mom, her friends and the warmth of the sun. If that wasn't enough, she has to deal with the curiosity of Forks' small town residents and the bizarre attentions of a strange and strangely beautiful boy.

All choices have consequences. The consequences of Bella's decision to live in Forks include dealing with a lot of rain, small school politics and falling in love with a vampire. Your choices have consequences, too, inevitably falling into your life like rain in Seattle. What you do with the results of your choices is another decision. The consequence of each choice affects the next choice you get to make.

It's been said that the only certainties in life are death and taxes. I would add "choices" to the list—of that I am certain. Well, that and the fact that all our choices have outcomes that we will have to deal with sooner or later.

Bella made an altruistic choice to live with her father while she finished high school. This choice set her on a path she could never have imagined back in sunny Arizona. She never expected to meet a guy she would fall in love with. She seriously never imagined that he would not be human.

You made choices this morning that set the tone for your day. Some choices were intentional. Others you may not have carefully considered, but rather made out of habit. You chose when to get out of bed, whether or not to eat breakfast, to go out or stay home and to pick up this book. Each of those choices influenced, to a certain degree, what happened next.

Some "choices" we make from habit, without even thinking about our actions. One of my friends has eaten Cheerios for breakfast for as long as she can remember. I predict she probably always will. I doubt she expects that tomorrow they will taste any differently. Cheerios taste like Cheerios. You wouldn't expect one day for them to taste like pineapples. But do you sometimes wish that something would break you out of your routine? Do you ever feel that it is impossible to change—that you have no choice? Do you "play the victim" rather than make changes that could improve your life?

Perhaps now is the time to quote Albert Einstein: "Insanity is doing the same thing over and over again and expecting different results."

Have you been thinking that perhaps it is time for a change?

Not all of us get to literally pack up and move to small, misty, Pacific Northwestern towns (or away from, if you're already there). But all of us have choices.

In the biblical book of Ruth, a young woman faces an unbearable loss and makes an unbelievable choice—one that makes Bella's sacrifice for her mother look like a choice between cinnamon and mint toothpaste. By the fifth verse of Ruth, chapter 1, our title character is a young widow. By verse 16 she has decided to travel with her mother-in-law, Naomi, to a foreign land, rather than stay with her family. You see, Naomi was an Israelite, as had been her husband and sons. They had been living in Moab due to a drought in Israel. Now that the drought was over, and with no family left in Moab, Naomi decides to return to Israel.

Naomi thought it was ridiculous for Ruth to follow her to Israel and tried to talk her into staying home, like her sister-in-law. At least in her homeland Ruth would be surrounded with the gods she grew up with and family to take care of her. But Ruth wouldn't hear it and said, "No. Your family is my family now, and the God you serve is now the God I serve. I want to be buried next to you and no one but God Himself is going to keep me from taking care of you until you die."

How do you refuse that? So Naomi says, "Eh. Whatever. Let's go." They begin the long trudge back to Israel, to Naomi's hometown of Bethlehem.

What an unbelievable, self-sacrificing choice! Is there any way Ruth could have expected anything good from her choice, really? She and her mother-in-law were both penniless widows. Where they were going, Ruth would be a cultural outsider and outcast because she was from Moab, an enemy nation to Israel. Bella may have felt like a freak in her new hometown, but Ruth could truly expect to be ostracized. As a widow she was a societal burden, and she was a foreigner to boot. Naomi could only hope that the tradition of distant relatives caring for widows was still an ongoing practice. She had no other way of supporting herself and her daughter-in-law.

Ruth gave up a likely second marriage and a lifetime of the familiar with her choice. However the old, dead idols with the same old, dead promises just didn't appeal to her as much as Naomi's God did, He Who could split oceans with a word and herd a nation through the barren desert. As it turns out, that God of miracles and wonders had a plan for our selfless heroine.

One form of Social Security available to widows such as Ruth and Naomi was the practice of gleaning. Biblical law said farmers should intentionally leave some of their crops in the field for widows and orphans to gather. In Bethlehem, Ruth immediately got to work gathering food to keep herself and her mother-in-law alive. The field she randomly chose just happened to belong to a wealthy man named Boaz, who was related to Naomi's dead husband.

When Boaz came to the field to supervise his workers, he noticed Ruth on the edges, picking up grain the harvesters had left behind. He inquired about her. His foreman told him all about Ruth and Naomi. He described how Ruth worked hard all day, taking only one short rest in the shade.

Bethlehem back in the day must have been a lot like Forks! Everyone knew Ruth had come with Naomi, and now they were getting a glimpse of who she really was. And who was Ruth? She was a hard worker, committed to making the best of her circumstances.

Can you see where this is heading? (Even with the spoiler alert, you really need to read the whole Book of Ruth. So worth it …) Boaz is impressed with what he hears and goes to speak with Ruth.

"Look," he says. "Stay in my fields with my servant girls. I've told the workers not to harass you in any way, and also that you have my permission to drink from the water jars they have filled."

Ruth is overwhelmed and bows deeply to express her gratitude. She asks why he would even notice her, since she was a negative balance in the social standing scale.

Boaz replies that he'd heard what she had done for Naomi, and that he could witness what she was doing now. He then pronounced a blessing over her, announcing that the God of Israel would richly reward her.

Wow! For making the tough but correct choice, Ruth has been noticed and recognized by this powerful and generous man. And his blessing on her is that she be honored by the Lord, the God of Israel, under Whose wings she had taken refuge. I love that Boaz recognized that her choice was truly about God. Offering Naomi comfort and companionship was a side benefit to pursuing a closer relationship to the one, true God she'd come to know through her now dead husband.

So after Boaz's kind words, Ruth went home to Naomi and reported on her day. Naomi was ecstatic with the news and told Ruth to stick close to Boaz's servant girls until the end of the harvest season.

And, Naomi began to plan …

Turns out Boaz held a unique legal standing in Old Testament law. Land was not permanently negotiable: it could be leased for as long as 70 years, but it belonged forever to the family it was assigned to when the Nation of Israel finally completed the Exodus and settled in Canaan. Because Ruth's husband and his brother were dead, there was no one to inherit the land—so someone called a *kinsman-redeemer* had to step in and make sure the land didn't leave the family by marrying Ruth and giving her a child. Boaz happened to be second in line. But he was first on Naomi's wish list for her beloved daughter-in-law, Ruth.

In Ruth Chapter 3, Naomi had Ruth subtly declare her preference for the older Boaz, and remind him he had the power to redeem the property and marry her in the process. Boaz, already impressed with her work ethic and dedication to Naomi, was now personally flattered that she would choose him over someone younger. He promises he will become her *kinsman redeemer*, in spite of the fact that there was someone more eligible in the eyes of the law.

Boaz quickly clears that hurdle, and Naomi's plan is rewarded. Boaz and Ruth marry and they are blessed with a son, whom they name Obed. Naomi becomes a grandmother and lives a long life in her homeland, surrounded by loved ones.

And, it gets better! Obed became grandfather to King David. David was ultimately an ancestor to Jesus Christ Himself. Ruth's unlikely choice earned her a mention in Matthew Chapter 1, verse 5, and she is honored forever in the genealogy of Jesus, Whose ultimately self-sacrificing choice makes life not only bearable but richly rewarding as well.

Another one of the most famous Biblical "moving to a new home" stories starts in a desert and includes a couple of amazing events involving water ... the story of moving to the Promised Land.

Moses hears God in a burning bush. He takes on the most powerful leader of the not-free world, leads a million people out of Egypt and wanders through the desert for 40 years. Finally he turns over leadership to Joshua, his first in command, just before the Israelites cross into the Promised Land. Moses dies before they enter the Promised Land. (Due to his own obedience issues he didn't get to go along ... but that's another chapter altogether.)

Joshua takes over and, following Moses' advice, he successfully conquers Canaan and establishes the Nation of Israel on the shores of the Mediterranean Sea. If you read the Book of Joshua, chapter 23, you will find that Joshua calls a family meeting. Joshua is one of two men still living who walked out of Egypt: the rest of that generation died in the desert. Joshua and Caleb lived to see this day because they believed God's promises. So Joshua causes the assembled people to remember their history—and with that in mind, asks them to make a choice. In chapter 24, beginning with verse 15, is that great challenge to the people: "Choose ye this day whom you will serve ... but as for me and my household, we will serve the Lord."

So, yeah, tough choices are challenging. It is difficult to be the new girl when you hate being the center of attention. It is hard to walk away from a particular career for the sake of your small children. Yet the promise of redemption when our choices are influenced by our sense of God's purpose is an irresistible call to untold adventure, if we will only listen.

We know by the end of *Twilight*—and especially at the end of *Breaking Dawn*—that Bella has no regrets about her choice to leave hot, sunny Arizona for the constant rain of Washington. She found a treasure worth more than 360 days of sun a year. The reward we obtain is even greater when we make Godly choices.

Of all the choices you make, can you think of one that has a greater impact than deciding to commit your life to the God Who redeemed Ruth and led the Israelites to the Promised Land? To the God Who, through Ruth, brought about your salvation through Christ? I pray that you will choose to allow Jesus Christ to lead you into the next adventure in your life. Like Bella, know that the decisions you make will change your life! Choose this day whom you will serve.

Chapter Worksheet

Suggested Group Activity
The Family Dinner Table

This is a good "ice breaker" for a group whose members don't know one another very well. It is non-threatening and a great way to introduce folks to one another.

Give each person paper and crayons. Have everyone draw a picture of the family dinner table from sometime in his or her early childhood. (They can choose the year!) Allow about 3-5 minutes to do this. Drawing skills are not required. Ask them to show who sat where, what the table looked like—anything particular they remember.

You can choose to have each person "present" their picture to the group or do this in groups of 2-4, depending on how much time you have. Everyone should give full attention to the presenter; no questions are asked. The presenter chooses how much to share. You, as the leader, might choose to go first to make everyone feel at ease.

Questions for Group Discussion

- Recall your own experiences of moving to a new home. What do you most remember?

- What did you find most surprising or what unexpected joy did you find?

- What "moving to a new home" stories from the Bible do you recall?

- Ruth's choice to move with Naomi was an act of faith. When have you had to make a choice as an act of faith, not assured of the outcome?

- Describe a "coming home to God" experience in your life.

CHAPTER 2

Gravity Moves

GRAVITY MOVES. **UNLESS ONE** is familiar with theories of relativity that suggest the speed of gravitational waves is equal to the speed of light—or you have read the *Twilight* series—the term *gravity moves* is rather peculiar.

In the *Twilight* series, the phrase "when gravity moves" refers to Jacob Black's description of his experience of imprinting on Bella and Edward's daughter, Renesmee. Following imprinting, Renesmee holds the earth together for Jacob—much like the force of gravity. Jacob is a *shape-shifter*, or werewolf, and will become whatever Renesmee needs. The act of imprinting is involuntary for shape-shifters. The reference infers that it is no longer gravity holding Jacob to the Earth but rather Renesmee, the "imprintee."

In scientific terms, *imprinting* refers to the phenomenon of newborn animals following and becoming socially bonded with the first moving object they encounter in a critical period. In humans, this process is believed to begin in the womb as the unborn baby learns to recognize its parents' voices. In both animals and humans, offspring acquire behavioral characteristics from those raising them: this is called *filial imprinting*.

> **God's love is less like Edward's— who admits he constantly battles with his essentially selfish nature— and more like that of Quil, who imprinted on young Claire.**

Scripture reveals God's "imprinting" on His creation. The opening verses of the Old Testament begin the story. Check this out: In Genesis 1:26-31, after each of the first five days of making something out of nothing, the Creator looks at what has been accomplished and sees that "it is good." Then, on the sixth day, God makes humankind. We are created in the image of God and God breathes into us the very breath of life. Talk about imprinting! When the Creator gets done and looks at the results, Scripture says: "God saw all that was made, and it was very good." Dude, we're *very good!* God thinks we rock. God blesses all of creation with affirmations of goodness.

One of the shortest verses in the Bible and the first to be memorized in Sunday School is "God is love." What does it mean? Have you ever thought about being imprinted with

God's love, from birth? God's intent for human beings—from the very beginning—is to love and be loved. God desires to live in harmony and union with us. The theological concept of the Trinity provides an example of this union.

A Trinitarian theology of the Godhead includes God the Creator, Jesus Christ the Redeemer and the Holy Spirit, the Renewer. But, you know what? That was not enough. God, the Creator, longs for His children's love in return. The imprint of God on each person identifies us all as children of God.

God's love is less like Edward's—who admits he constantly battles with his essentially selfish nature—and more like that of Quil Ateara. Quil is one of the wolf pack and the one who imprinted on the young Claire. Bella's friend and wolf pack member, Jacob Black, explained how this kind of love does not take advantage of its imprintee, but rather becomes exactly what the loved one needs at each stage of life.

While Claire is young, Quil will be the best, most attentive caregiver any child could need. As she grows he will be her best friend and confidant, giving sound advice and exceptional guidance. When she is an adult, she will learn to love him with the depth and virtue with which he has loved her.

Just so, God's love provides what we need in order to mature into the people of God. When we are new believers, God nurtures us as a parent protects and teaches a child. Jeremiah 31:3 and 9 tell us that the extent of God's love is everlasting. God teaches us with "loving kindness." Picture a doting father bent over at the waist, helping a toddler learn how to walk.

When we first come to know God, we have to start with the basics. Like babies, the Apostle Peter in 1 Peter 2:2-3 tells us to crave pure spiritual milk. To grow in faith, seek out good teachers who will help you understand the Bible and who will encourage you.

Hebrews 5:12-14 assures us that as we pursue a relationship with God and grow in spiritual wisdom, God will nurture us, bringing new opportunities to experience and allowing us to practice grace. In fact, growth is expected of us; otherwise we will be stunted and immature in our spirituality with the potential to cause more harm than good. If so, we have no one to blame but ourselves. If you are yearning for more—to grow in faith—then prayerfully seek spiritual teachers and communities of faith. Spend time reading, not only Scripture but also great writings from saints and "spiritual giants" of the faith. Find a mentor and spiritual guide to nurture and encourage you on your faith journey.

In Jeremiah, God calls Israel "Ephraim." Ephraim was Jacob's favorite grandson, one who eventually became one of the 12 tribes of Judah. Here God is using his name as a nickname, more or less, for the Nation of Israel. Perhaps this is because, historically, Ephraim—of all the tribes—was most likely to act like a spoiled child. Yet God loves this headstrong nation-state with a depth that is nearly incomprehensible. It is that same depth of crazy love He lavishes on us.

Each of us is imprinted with the love of God. The end goal is to bring us to complete spiritual maturity. God is raising up for Himself a bride, spotless and without flaw. Quil will do anything to protect little Claire, to help her grow up to be the best she can be in hopes that she will, in turn, choose him when she is grown. We see Jesus in Ephesians 5:25-27 doing the exact same thing. He provides Scripture and wise teachers to instruct and motivate us. Jesus stands at God's right hand to cheer us on, while providing the Holy Spirit to constantly guide and encourage us.

In Ephesians 5:25-27, emphasis is placed on "washing with water through the Word." Again and again the Word of God, the Bible, is emphasized as most necessary for spiritual growth. Prayer is our venue for communicating with God and receiving guidance and encouragement. In fact, these two are sides of the same coin: each is equally necessary to grow in spiritual maturity. Dig into the Word and find teachers or books that will help you understand God's great love poem to the world. Pray for understanding every time you open the Bible.

Everything in the Old Testament can be understood as a prequel to Jesus and His sacrifice on the cross. Since Genesis, when Eve and Adam decided their will was better than God's, there has been a rift in the universe. It is often through stories or pictures that we can best understand concepts such as sin. The temptation story of Adam and Eve reveals how our childish impulses to do things our own way separate us from God's eternal love. Adam and Even walked daily in the Garden with God prior to their disobedience. Afterward, they felt the pain of separation.

We might not really know what we are missing, so God pursues us and plants in our hearts a deep longing for communion. We have been imprinted by God from creation. Jesus, on the cross, is God's great gift of love. Jesus' life, death and resurrection reverse the results of Eve's sin. We are no longer bound to the patterns of behavior we inherited from Adam and Eve. We are no longer exiled from God. God's design is to raise us from spiritual infants to spiritual maturity; as believers who will change the world. We are meant to usher in the Kingdom of God and to reflect God's goodness and design.

Echoes of God's perfect design reverberate everywhere. In the creation story, at the end of each day, God looks at creation and declares it is "good." Who hasn't recognized the glorious goodness of God while viewing the majesty of the mountains, the beauty of a meadow overflowing with wild-flowers or the peacefulness of a sunrise at the dawning of a new day?

Occasionally, we glimpse examples of humans acting out God's unconditional love and intent.

More than 20 years ago in Florida, a woman had to deal with the unbearable loss of her daughter at the hands of a drunk driver. Instead of carrying that rage, bitterness and pain around in her heart for the rest of her life, she sought out the young offender in jail. He, understandably, did not want to see her. Perhaps he couldn't bear the thought of seeing her pain in real time, face to face like that. The jailer insisted he meet her. To his immense surprise, she forgave him. And more, she asked him to become her son to replace the daughter she had lost.

Can you imagine so great a love that it would offer not only forgiveness but also restoration as a member of the family? What a world-spinning concept that must have been for that young man. Not only could he maybe, someday, possibly make up for his horrible sin against this woman; he was the one who seemed to win the most from the exchange! God stands, too, waiting for us to come out of our prison cells and receive His offer of unconditional love and entry into His family.

As Jacob Black so succinctly explained, it is difficult to resist that level of commitment and adoration.

When you allow gravity to move and let God become the center of your world, all other experiences and relationships will be so much better—and richer—as a result.

Chapter Worksheet

Jeremiah 1:4-8 reinforces the concept that God knew you even before you were formed in your mother's womb. You arrive on earth "imprinted" with the love of God. Read these verses aloud as a group.

Also read Jeremiah 29:11-14. What reassurance comes from knowing that the God of Creation has a plan for us—and from the promise that when we seek God with all our heart, we will find Him?

Suggested Group Activity
Drawing a map or timeline of your spiritual journey

If you have the time and interest, give each person a sheet of newsprint and markers (or crayons). Ask everyone to make a map or timeline of his or her spiritual journey, from birth to the present. Remind them there is no "right" or "wrong" way to do this. This activity will tap into a different part of the brain and unconscious to reveal each person's spiritual journey. Some will draw pictures; others might choose a very linear chart with notations. Encourage participants to be creative. Ask them to think about significant experiences, people, ideas, moments, revelations—anything that has been part of their spiritual growth. Included may be times of illness or crisis that led to a greater understanding of faith. The expression of each life's journey will be as unique as the journey itself. Allow at least 15 minutes for this activity.

If possible, tape each person's paper up on the wall. Allow time for each person to show what he or she drew. They can tell as much or as little as they choose. No one can make comments about someone else's drawing. In addition, the leader should ask the group members to listen carefully, with their hearts and minds, as each person shares. They will receive insight into how they might best mentor and encourage this person in faith.

You might have to set time limits for each person or devote a separate meeting just for doing this activity. It is a wonderful process not only for individuals to reflect on their own journey, but also for group members to become better acquainted with one another.

Close by reading Revelations 21:1-5, 9-11.

That's us! Shining with jewels; pure as crystal; the crown of the Kingdom of God. I find that supremely motivating, to be held and admired as a precious jewel in the Hand of God. God continues to "imprint," transforming and making all things new.

Questions for Group Discussion

- Where in creation do you see the "imprint" of God's love?

- Who has been a spiritual mentor, protector or guide to you? Name either that person's characteristics or the ways that he or she encouraged and nurtured you on your faith journey.

- What experiences in your life have made you feel like "gravity moved?"

- Relate a time in your life when you were aware of God's imprinting—or of how you have experienced God's "imprinting" of love.

CHAPTER 3

You Won't Hurt Me

IN THE MOVIE *TWILIGHT*, Bella goes to meet Edward's family and to see his house for the first time. After a round of awkward introductions, Edward gives Bella a tour that includes his room on the top floor, which opens up to the canopy of evergreens surrounding the house.

The conversation turns to trust. Bella claims she is not afraid of Edward. He takes this as a challenge. Bella gasps as, in one swift movement, Edward swings her onto his back and leaps out the window. He is halfway up an ancient tree before he asks, "Do you trust me?"

"In theory …" she replies, her voice shaky.

"Then close your eyes!" Edward says, before taking her on a treetop adventure she had never imagined possible.

Perhaps you are at the same point in your relationship with God. You know God loves you—the question is, how much do you trust in return? Is there anything you would not put into God's hands? Why not?

It was a dream job: four-day workweeks with alternating two- and four-day weekends, great pay, prestige, a corporate ladder to climb and a boss who encouraged upward mobility. The work was exactly what I studied for in college and a logical outgrowth of previous work experience.

So what was my problem? I had constant stomachaches. It took all of the four-day weekend for the tension in my jaw to relax. Each day ended with a headache and a dread of the next day. I was beginning to hate work, and my feelings about work were poisoning friendships and professional relationships. Eventually, I was given an ultimatum: suck it up and do my job, or resign before they fired me. Much time was spent in tears, crying out to God and asking why my plans were unraveling so spectacularly.

The key was in that prayer. Notice I asked God about *my* plans. I graduated from college with hopes of being the next Lois Lane. When journalism lost its luster, I moved into corporate public relations. Initially, I thought I had it made. All those great points, plus health and dental? All I needed now was Prince Charming!

Within months the stress began to wear on me. I began to see that I didn't know myself very well at all. Apparently, I'm not corporate material. I wasn't fulfilled being just an anonymous cog in a big machine. That was not who God made me. Go figure. The realization was painful. If I wasn't who I thought I was, then who was I?

One evening in prayer with a trusted group of friends, I had what can only be described as a vision. It was so clear:

I stood on the edge of a cliff, like Bella cliff-diving in *New Moon*, except in my vision there was no rain. The bright sun shone on tropical foliage behind me, and the water was that beautiful, clear blue-green I'd only seen in ads for Caribbean resorts. And—as if He were whispering in my ear—God gave me a choice: I could stay where I was, on the uncomfortable edge of the cliff, clinging to the vines and struggling for toeholds; or I could jump, and trust that I would either survive the fall or learn to fly. The choice was mine.

Dear readers, I jumped. I turned in my resignation without a clue as to what I'd do next. In true-to-form, miraculous fashion, God came through. At a fraction of my former pay—and even less prestige and no chance of upward mobility—I accepted the position of Youth Leader in a small church in a small town, on the opposite side of the state. You will probably not be surprised to learn it was one of the most rewarding periods of my life. I truly learned to fly on wings of faith. That leap was a first step that laid the foundation for the rest of my life. It led to this moment, to the writing of this book and to the hope that your life will be changed, too.

> Similarly, we are called to step out in faith, onto the promises of God.

So, this has what to do with Bella clinging to Edward's back 20 feet off the ground?

One echoing theme in *Twilight* is trust. Bella has faith that Edward will not kill her, either intentionally or accidentally. The Cullens (excepting Rosalie, of course) trust that Bella will not expose them for what they are.

Trust and faith help us do what is otherwise impossible. Bella should have run away from the terrifying power Edward held. Yet her trust in his love held her, a trust that would be called into question and tested soon enough. Similarly, we are called to step out in faith, onto the promises of

God. Each time we exercise that choice—each time our faith is tested—we grow stronger; we become closer to understanding God and closer to understanding who God created us to be.

Of all the stories of exercising trust, Abraham's moves me the most. Again and again in Abraham's very long life, God makes outrageous promises and asks for outrageous actions. When Abraham was about 75 years old, God asked him to pack up everything he had and move away from everything he'd ever known, with nothing but a promise found in Genesis 12:2-3. It's a fantastic promise to be sure, that Abraham will be the founder of a great nation and that every nation will be blessed through him. There was no MapQuest, and God didn't include a GPS in the bargain.

Nonetheless, what does Abraham do? He breaks camp, tosses his wife, Sarah, on a camel, rounds up his nephew for company and moves away. When he arrives at Shechem, just north of modern-day Jerusalem, God says, "To your offspring I will give this land." Imagine that! Two hundred years before his grandson, Jacob, and his 12 sons end up in Egypt due to a famine, almost 700 years before the Israelites break free from Egypt to complete the Exodus and 2,000 years before the final clause is fulfilled through Christ, God gives Abraham a glimpse of his plan.

Twenty-five years after that declaration, 90-year-old Sarah has given up hope and considers the promise a cosmic joke. Suddenly—amazingly—the promise is fulfilled. Sarah and Abraham have a son they name Isaac. Isaac—whose name means "laughter"—is truly the pride and joy of this old couple. But God has a question for Abraham, a test in Genesis 22:1-14. God asks Abraham to take Isaac for a little trip—and once he gets there, to sacrifice his son on an altar.

What?!

Sacrifice the son of the promise? The son of his old age? His heart's joy and delight? Is this the God we are expected to follow?

Abraham apparently thought so, since he immediately saddled up his donkey, called two servants and gathered Isaac, too. He also chopped up some wood for the sacrifice and packed it for the trip. This old man who had waited 100 years for this son *cut the wood himself.*

Can you imagine what went through his head with each swing of the axe?

"I love my son."

"Why are You asking this of me?"

"Yet, You've never let me down."

"You made promises of the future to be fulfilled through Isaac!"

"Your promise of Isaac himself proved trustworthy and true."

"I don't understand."

"Yet, I will trust You."

After three days of travel, Abraham and Isaac arrived at the mountain. Abraham instructed the servants to stay behind with the donkey. He told them he and Isaac would walk a ways to worship God and that both of them would return. He had Isaac carry the wood while he carried a knife and coals to start the fire.

Isaac, of course, eventually asked the question that must have been bothering him for some time: "Dad, where's the lamb?"

I can only imagine Abraham, overwhelmed with emotion as he answered that God Himself would provide the offering. Yet as they trudged up the mountain together, no sacrifice appeared, no matter how hard they looked.

At the top Abraham built an altar, piling stones just so and arranging the wood. I imagine Isaac helped out. We have no indication that he was a sulking or rebellious child. Eventually the altar was complete and Abraham could not delay his obedience any longer. He tied up his son like he had so many sheep before, and laid him on the altar. He must have been weeping when he picked up the knife for the fatal cut, but just as he moved in for the final act of obedience a voice literally cried out from the heavens, calling Abraham's name.

Can't you just hear Abraham's voice crack when he replies, "Here I am?" The emotion that must have flooded him!

The voice, the Angel of God, tells Abraham not to harm the boy. The test was complete. Abraham was willing to go as far as to give his son, his only son, back to God.

But the question remains: Why? Why would God insist Abraham place on the altar and almost destroy the most precious object in his life? Did God need proof that Abraham feared Him? Or did Abraham need a reality check? Perhaps, as Isaac grew up, Abraham thought everything was complete. Perhaps he had become complacent, satisfied with his place and sure his work was done. Had Isaac become a little too much of Abraham's pride and joy, when God should have always remained at the top of the list?

I have never had to place one of my children on the altar, and I pray I never have to. But throughout my Christian walk I have had to weigh my values. Time and again God has asked me to place attitudes, desires, careers and identity on the altar. Sometimes I get to take them off again. But in this process of learning obedience, I find I sometimes become complacent, materialistic, or distracted in one form or another. God often needs to do something drastic to get my attention and get me on track again.

Perhaps you are struggling now. Did you notice Abraham's response when God called? "Here I am," he replied. I challenge you: reply to God with a simple, "Here I am." See if the way isn't made clear to you when you listen for the Creator's voice. Just as Abraham put his complete trust in God, be assured that you, too, can trust in the Almighty to save.

> And Abraham lifted up his eyes, and looked, and behold behind [him] a ram caught in a thicket by his horns: and Abraham went and took the ram, and offered him up for a burnt offering in the stead of his son.
>
> —*Genesis 22:13-14*

Chapter Worksheet

Suggested Group Activity
Guided Imagery Prayer

This prayer experience taps into additional areas of our brains beyond reason and logic, and into intuition and deeper ways of "knowing."

Ask participants to let themselves relax, allowing images to flow freely into their minds and hearts. To be effective, you need to create a peaceful, undisturbed atmosphere. Close the door so you won't be disturbed. Turn off the lights and light a candle. Play peaceful, meditative music softly in the background. Instruct participants to find a comfortable position, to sit or even lie down on the floor. They may want to move further apart so as not to interfere with one another's thoughts and prayers. Remind them there is no right or wrong way, and that they should just allow whatever pictures come to mind into their thoughts as you guide the prayer images.

Begin by asking everyone to close their eyes and slowly breathe in and out, taking very deep breaths. (Most, after three deep breaths, will be relaxed and focused.) Remind them to let tension flow out of their bodies as they slowly breathe in and out.

Read the following very slowly, allowing long pauses for the participants to see where their hearts take them. The pauses can be 30 seconds to 60, although this will feel like a long time to you!

- Picture yourself in a sacred place.
- A place full of light and peace.
- Look around.
- What do you see?
- What do you smell?
- What do you hear?
- Before you is an altar.
- It is empty.
- What is it made of?
- How big is it?
- You hear the voice of God asking you to put something on the altar.
- What is it?
- Accept the first thing that comes to mind.
- Don't try to manipulate this.
- If at first you don't know, wait and it will come to you.
- *(Give them a longer time of silence.)*
- What do you do?
- *(Give them a couple minutes of silence.)*
- Now, I invite you to come back to this time and place.
- Relax in God's love.
- Feel God's presence deep inside you.

- Just enjoy experiencing God's unconditional love.
- Next, invite someone into your heart.
- You will know who it is.
- Picture this person in God's presence with you.
- You and God love this person.
- *(Long pause)*
- Now let that image go.
- Finally, I invite you to rest in God's presence.
- Together, let us say the Lord's Prayer.
- *(Any prayer the group is familiar with will do.)*
- Amen.

If group members haven't opened their eyes, invite them to do so.

The group may want to share with one another the images they experienced during this prayer exercise. You could do this in smaller groups, depending on how much time you have.

Questions for Debriefing the Guided Imagery

- How would you describe this prayer experience?

- What did the altar look like?

- Did you know immediately what you needed to put on the altar? Were you surprised by what came to mind?

- What did you do? Do you know why?

- How did you feel?

Going Deeper
Bible Study

There are few more profound pictures of trust than that of sheep with their shepherd. In mountainous regions, sheep left to their own devices soon come to an early end. As a whole, they are defenseless from predators, very poor foragers and hopeless navigators.

Read Psalm 23:1 and Isaiah 53:6 to find who or what David identifies himself with in the world's most popular psalm.

It's not that sheep are malicious. Not even in cartoons are sheep portrayed as wicked; they're just clueless, and it gets them into trouble. None of us are that innocent. We've all been wicked. Occasionally we are simply clueless, stumbling around and, like sheep, tumbling into pits.

How fortunate are we, then, to have a Good Shepherd? God is crazy gracious and crazy in love with us sheep. He has no intentions of leaving us to our own devices if we are willing to follow His voice.

Read Jeremiah 29:11 (yes, again).

What does God have for you? Write it down.

And that's a good thing, right?

But, you ask, what do God's plans look like? And how do you begin to find them?

Read Psalm 23:2-3. Write down the four things God does.

Using these two verses, each situation can be seen as one of four options.

Are you in a place where you need to rest and absorb His goodness for you? Those green pastures are places of learning and gathering strength.

Are you being moved on to the next stage in life? If you are moving in God's will, there is refreshment along the way.

Are you in the midst of a spiritual challenge, needing to turn to God for renewal and revival? Only God can relieve the weariness that sometimes makes our souls feel heavy.

Is God calling you to an action bigger than yourself? Everything leads to this—doing that which brings glory to God's name. It's not just that God has been grooming you to use you, but that you will be most fulfilled when you do what God has designed you to do.

These verses capture the cyclical nature of life. As flocks of sheep are rotated through various fields during the year we, also, rotate through different phases of our faith journeys.

Questions for Group Discussion

- Think about three persons you would trust your life with. What qualities or characteristics do they share? Why would you trust them with your life?

- Who did you identify with most in the story of Abraham—Sarah, Isaac, Abraham, Abraham's servants or God—and why?

- Have you ever had a "leap of faith" experience? What made it difficult or easy?

- When do you find it difficult to trust in God?

- What reassures you or helps you trust God?

CHAPTER 4

You Don't See Yourself Very Clearly

DIE-HARD *TWILIGHT* FANS know a secret: *Midnight Sun*, an unfinished fifth novel written from Edward's point of view, was leaked and has now been made available by the author on her website. For the first time, readers get a peek into Edward's mind, as the previous novels were all narrated by Bella.

We learn that Edward finds Bella especially attractive—and not just to his vampire appetites. But Bella has a poor self-image. As Edward observes her, he finds that she is sensitive, thoughtful, intelligent and beautiful. He is completely astounded to learn that she thinks of herself as "ordinary" in the worst sense of the word. Edward believes her very existence justifies the world.

What about you? Do you see yourself as ordinary? Who determines the words you use to describe yourself? Have you filtered your self-value through the eyes of someone else? Have you tried to see yourself through the eyes of God?

So, what is it that attracted Edward to Bella in the first place, aside from her appealing scent? Once he got past seeing her as a meal and observed her as a person, Edward noted characteristics about Bella that he found deeply appealing.

Edward's list of Bella's beautiful traits included not only a perceptive and intelligent mind but also a selfless nature. She was responsible, brave, mature, kind, lovely and intriguing. In short, he concluded that she was good and that he loved her for these intangible things. Only after Edward was completely in love with Bella's inner self did he realize he found her breathtakingly beautiful on the outside as well.

Hmmmm ... inner beauty. What a concept! This concept is completely alien in Western culture, where we seem so driven by outward appearances.

It's kind of like the inverse of the redneck bumper sticker: "Beauty is only skin deep, but ugly goes all the way to the bone." In truth, beauty begins inside and can't help but seep through and color how others see us.

Maybe that's why Edward never found other vampires like Rosalie or Tanya attractive. He was well aware of their vanity and it tarnished their physical beauty. I wonder who our beauty queens would be if our inner selves were as apparent as our physical appearances? Conversely, I wonder who would suddenly lose his or her luster in the media spotlight?

You know Edward's insight has nothing on God's. Psalm 139:1-4 describes how thoroughly God knows us. Our

Creator God knows what we are doing, when we are doing it and why we are motivated to act the way we do.

I don't care what your name is—your thoughts are not immune to God's listening mind. We cannot hide the contradiction between what we think and the words we allow to slip out of our mouths. Read Psalm 139:13-16 to comprehend the depth of God's understanding of us.

God knows how to read what you're thinking because your mind—and how it works—was His creation. Your Creator God knows why you think what you think. It is comforting to me to know that there is nothing wrong with my mind that the Lord cannot fix, and that sometimes, thinking differently from others is, in fact, God's design to start with.

This beautiful psalm ends with a request:

> Search me, O God, and know my heart: try me,
> and know my thoughts:
> And see if [there be any] wicked way in me, and
> lead me in the way everlasting.
> —*Psalm 139:23-24*

Interestingly, the Hebrew translation for *the way* in Psalm 139 can refer to a physical direction or path, but it can also apply to moral character. The Hebrew word for *everlasting* doesn't just stretch ahead of us, but into the unending past as well. God is capable and willing to hook us into eternity, if we are only willing to let that happen.

So, God can read our thoughts from afar. This God of the universe made us and knows what we're capable of, and whether we're living up to it or not. And God is capable of searching our thoughts and correcting them. This God Who knows us inside and out loves us eternally—not based on our merit, skills, physical beauty or status, but simply because He is love.

Does the Bible speak of feminine beauty? Quite a bit, actually. In one analogy, God warns Israel that it is acting like a beautiful woman in danger of destroying herself by sleeping around with anyone who looks at her. God is particularly explicit regarding this behavior in the Book of Ezekiel.

In the New Testament, in 1 Peter 3:3-4, women are warned not to rely on physical beauty or fashionable accessories. It is a reminder that beauty is not what we put on, whether it be eye shadow or designer jeans. Amazingly, the "unfading beauty of a gentle and quiet spirit" has a testimonial advertisement. In the next few verses of 1 Peter, we learn that when we put our hope in God, we are Sarah's daughters. Sarah was Abraham's wife and was renowned for her beauty.

In Genesis 12, we read that Abraham (then still known as Abram) and Sarah (still Sarai) traveled to Egypt due to a famine. Abram was between the ages of 75 and 86, and Sarai was 10 years younger than he. So, you've got to figure she's at least 65. In Genesis 12:11-12, Abram is so afraid that he will be killed so Sarai would be free to be taken as wife by someone else that he asks her to tell everyone she is his sister. Technically it wasn't a lie, as they were half-siblings—ewww, I know—but it was a critical omission of truth, and God does set him straight. Abram's fears were realized when his "sister" was taken by a local king to be a member of his harem. Can you imagine? Now, I can get behind a beauty regimen that, at 65, incites men to kidnapping! Helen of Troy had nothing on Sarai!

Proverbs 31:10-31 is another passage full of descriptions of internal beauty. See how many of these characteristics line up with the admirable traits Edward saw in Bella: noble character, ambitiousness, intelligence, strength, wisdom, generosity, forward thinking, good humor and steadfastness. Pretty close, huh? Bonus question: If you want to snag an Edward, what should you be working on?

How do we reach that place of inner beauty that oozes out through our skin? Start with Romans 12:1 and spend time working on each verse, individually, until it becomes a part of who you are.

> ...present your bodies a living sacrifice, holy, acceptable unto God, [which is] your reasonable service. And be not conformed to this world: but be ye transformed by the renewing of your mind, that ye may prove what [is] that good, and acceptable, and perfect, will of God.

—Romans 12:1b-2a

There is a lot to unpack in those two sentences alone.

First, our bodies are not our own. My body has been given to God and I must treat it as such. What kind of clothes would I dress God in? Modest ones, to be sure. When I shop I am careful not to buy shirts that are too tight or too low cut, because being a walking, talking distraction is not pleasing to God. I remember that although I intend to be a beautiful 70-year-old (not there yet), I cannot dress like I'm still 16 (not there anymore). As a representative body of God, it is my responsibility to dress well: not in trash and not trashy. Is that difficult? Yes, sometimes it is, but that is my "living sacrifice." It is with this act of worship, of showing my love to God, that I turn my back on those cute little skirts because they would send the wrong message about whose I am and who I want to be.

The whole of Romans 12 is practical, feet-on-the-pavement-of-life advice on how to develop an inner beauty that is beyond value. Besides, I've witnessed time and time again that putting your trust in God and throwing your worries on Him is a great way to prevent wrinkles.

So, what about you? Are you ordinary? Are you beautiful? In whose estimation? What does God have to say about beauty? What does He value in us? How important is it to God that we feel good about ourselves? It's pretty important, actually. But the traditional understanding of self-esteem, feeling good about ourselves *just because,* is amazingly far from the kind of confidence God wants us to experience.

This is what God considers beautiful: humility (confidence properly placed in God) and obedience. Beauty is a choice. Choose to walk in humility before God and obey His commands so that you may live in victorious peace all the days of your life.

A parting bit of humor: At 20, a woman has the face God gave her. At 40, a woman has the face she has created. At 60, she has the face she deserves, no matter what she does.

Chapter Worksheet

Suggested Group Activity

Pass out pens and paper. Ask participants to make two lists. First, have them list at least 10 of their best qualities. Give participants time to complete this before you give the second assignment. The second assignment is to list what they think others would say were their 10 best qualities.

Ask these questions:

Which list was easier to complete and why?

What was different or similar between the two lists?

Questions for Group Discussion

• Why do we tend to "judge a book by its cover?"

• Tell about an experience when you totally misjudged someone based only on his or her outer appearance.

- When have you attempted to look at someone through the eyes of God, rather than just from your own perspective? What was the result? How did this change you?

- How does it change the way you live if God knows you inside and out?

CHAPTER 5

The Face of the Monster in Me

EDWARD AND BELLA FIRST meet in biology class. She is assigned the only empty seat, which happens to be next to Edward. In *Midnight Sun*, Edward explains that all the other humans had subconsciously avoided sitting next to him, somehow aware that he was not safe to be near. Unaware of the danger and without much of a choice, Bella sat down. Edward was ready to be polite—until he caught one whiff of her scent. The vampire nature he had worked 100 years to keep under control nearly burst out of him in a single violent attack.

All Bella knew was that this guy who had never said a word to her suddenly seemed to hate her. It was revealed through his body language and the revulsion on his face. Her eyes grew wide enough for him to see his reflection before she quickly looked away; Edward was shocked by what he saw there. He saw the monster he had dominated for decades trying to dominate him. It taunted him.

What forbidden action, attitude or desire taunts you?

It was wrong. So wrong. But it was who (or, more precisely, *what*) Edward was to want Bella in the worst imaginable way. Not as a person, a precious soul, but as a consumable commodity. She was something to be used up, emptied and tossed aside. It is the ultimate vanity that his physical need would trump her right to live. Fortunately for Bella, Edward retained just enough grip on this knowledge to restrain his inner nature. It was a nature that could tear its way out of him and into her, destroying more than just their two lives.

Don't think you can relate? Betcha can. ... How often do we use others? When is sexual intimacy merely about fulfilling one's own needs, rather than an act of love and devotion? When do we use someone else to promote our own career or success? When do we take more than we need at the expense of those who go without?

Once upon a time there were two brothers. They were as different as night and day. While both were farmers, they chose as different of paths as possible. Cain worked the land and made his living with his hands in the soil, raising and harvesting crops; Abel was a rancher, breeding and raising flocks of sheep.

In Genesis 4:4-5, each man offered a portion of his respective harvest to God. God looked at the men and at their offerings. Abel's offering was accepted, but Cain's was not.

Be sure to note that this was not about what each man was offering. The Lord looked at each individual and the attitude with which he made the offering. It quickly became obvious that Cain, who couldn't take a hint, had a serious attitude problem. The Hebrew word behind *very angry* in verse 5 is *charah*: "to be hot, furious, burn, become angry, be kindled." The English translation doesn't capture the depth of feeling in this word. It is a deep rage that Cain experienced when he realized God had more respect for his brother than for him. But rather than address the situation productively, he walked around sulking and fuming.

God was gracious and didn't not leave Cain to stumble around, trying to figure out what he'd done wrong and how to fix it. In verses 6 and 7, God went to Cain and even gave him specific directions. Did God reject Cain's offering arbitrarily? Had He already met His offering-per-day quota? No! God was trying to get Cain's attention. God was encouraging Cain to do the right thing. We don't know exactly what it was that Cain wasn't doing right. We don't know, for example, if he was cheating on his taxes, cheating on his wife or just a cheap miser with a miserable attitude. Whatever it was, though, was not a mystery to Cain—and he didn't want to change. So he plotted an easier way out. He killed his brother (Genesis 4:8).

The monster in Cain's mirror won. Cain had a chance to turn from evil purposes, but he chose not to fight them. Cain joined forces with the sin at his door and committed the first murder in history. Whatever he had been struggling with before seemed trivial; he was now in a place 100 times worse. His brother was dead. His parents were heartbroken. He was banished from the only home he'd ever known. He lived in fear that his brother's death would be avenged by his own murder.

The clearest definition of sin I've ever heard is "a deliberate disobedience to the known will of God." Sin is rebellion or disobedience to God, but ultimately it is about our relationship with God. Sin can also be defined as anything that comes between us and God. We learned in the creation story of Adam and Eve, the parents of Cain and Abel, that we have a choice. We have a choice: to choose sin or to choose a life walking daily with God. Sin drove Cain into exile. The results are the same for us. We, too, are driven by sin into exile from God, from one another and even from our true selves.

We have a natural urge and tendency to sin, just as the vampires of *Twilight*—whether they are Cullens or not—desire blood. This great God of love follows the rules of love; therefore, God gives us the freedom to choose. We become aware at a very young age of that tendency to choose self-interest over God's loving ways. The first time a playmate or sibling takes a toy from our hands we experience a sense of betrayal, of "being sinned against." It is usually only a short time later that we battle those exact tendencies in ourselves.

> For the wages of sin is death, but the gift of God
> is eternal life in Christ Jesus our Lord.
> —*Romans 6:23*

But there is victory available to us! Just as God encouraged Cain to master the sin that would master him, we also have that opportunity. It's called *salvation through grace*. It is giving ourselves over to the love of God through the saving power of Jesus Who already took on Himself the death sin brings to us.

Look up Romans 6:11-14 and read it out loud. I love the echo we hear at the end of that passage, the reverse of Genesis: Where sin would master Cain, it shall not master me, because I have offered my body to God through Christ and am now living under this grace. Oh, hallelujah! I am free!

Don't get me wrong. Life is full of struggles. I must constantly adjust my attitude, especially toward those nearest and dearest to me. Like Cain, my family often gets the worst of me. But *grace*. ... When God reminds me that my behavior is displeasing, I run back and accept correction because I know it is not only in my best interest, but in the interest of everyone I interact with as well.

It *is* possible, as this story shows, to live your life without violating one of the Ten Commandments and still be exiled from God. Cain was checked for his attitude. He did not sin until he killed his brother. You can memorize and live by Exodus 20:1-17, but until your inner motivations line up with your external actions, you live on the edge of the knife like Cain.

Jesus, in the Sermon on the Mount, goes into great detail concerning attitudes. Starting in Matthew Chapter 5, Jesus offers the Beatitudes. In poetic form, Jesus offers blessings that result from an attitude of the heart for those who follow God's ways of love. In Matthew 5:17 and going through 6:4, Jesus emphasizes the importance not only of action but also of attitude. It is wrong to commit adultery, but it is also wrong to lust after someone else. It is wrong to murder, but it is also wrong to stay angry. Read Matthew 5:23-24 and think about Cain. Before you can offer a sacrifice pleasing to God, your attitude needs to be in the right place.

God may have been asking Cain to do something as simple as asking his brother to forgive him for something he'd thoughtlessly done. Maybe it wasn't a slight thing at all. But because he stubbornly did not want to make it right, Cain ended up violating one of the best-known commandments of all: "Thou shall not kill."

Sin is not an arcane, dead concept without application, as much as our modern world would like to deny it. Sin is real, and it can have long-lasting consequences. But it is not undefeatable. Sometimes it takes outrageous efforts of personal strength and will—just as Edward fought back with every ounce of discipline he could muster in his desire for

Bella's blood. But we are not alone. The God who cheers us on to win also gives us strength in the fight when we pray and cling to grace.

Chapter Worksheet

Suggested Group Activity

Play quiet, meditative music in the background. You can light a candle on a table in the center of the group and begin with a simple prayer, asking the Holy Spirit to be present and to guide the group. Pass out pens and paper. Have each person write something he or she deeply regrets, something that needs forgiveness or a behavior he or she needs to change. Don't rush this; be comfortable with silence. Have group members fold their paper and write their name on the outside. Collect them and then randomly pass them out to the group members, being careful that no one receives his own paper. Be sure to tell them that **no one is to read the papers!**

Keep the music playing, and give these instructions to the group: One at a time, each person reads the name on the paper and invites the other person to join him or her at the center of the circle (where you have placed the candle and a waste receptacle). The person looks at the one who wrote the confession and, while ripping up the paper and putting it into the waste bin, says the following: "(Insert name), you are a beloved child of God. You are forgiven. Go, live in God's love." The entire group responds each time with, "You are forgiven indeed. Amen!"

Close with a prayer of pardon and affirmation.

Questions for Group Discussion

- Who has been most accepting and forgiving toward you when you acted less than your best self? How did this person show forgiveness and compassion?

- What do you struggle with most?

- How do you find your way back when you have done something wrong or sinned?

- Tell of an experience of God's grace and forgiveness.

CHAPTER 6

Emily's Ruined Face

IN *NEW MOON*, **BELLA** discovers that her best friend, Jacob, is a werewolf. Technically, as a member of the Quileute tribe, it's more of a shape-shifter thing. But the effect is about the same: he's a guy one minute, and then the next he's a really, really big wolf. And he's dangerous, not only to his enemies but also to anyone nearby when the wolf comes out. It's a terrifying thing, not just to witness but, as Jacob explains, to experience as well.

Jacob tells Bella he hates feeling out of control. He sees the damage that lack of control can cause when he looks at his friends, Sam and Emily. Emily was standing next to Sam once when he changed into a wolf, and now half of her face is scar tissue, shaped forever with huge claw marks.

We have seen the damage done by people who are out of control. Out of control drunk drivers kill people, out of control authorities ruin governments and out of control individuals ruin other people's lives. Are you really, fully, truly in control? Or do you sometimes worry that you are a danger to those you love?

I am my father's daughter. This is a good thing, most of the time. I'm proud of my father, Dale, and am pleased to be known as his daughter. For example, if there's someone at the edge of the swimming pool, I'm probably the one to "accidentally" bump him in. Putting things together with my hands, especially useful things, makes me happy. This will absorb my attention for hours, even while you hear me muttering about poorly drawn and written instructions. I love to laugh and have a goofy sense of humor—occasionally morbid—but humor nevertheless. I don't like doing things halfway. And I've been known to knock a perfectly innocent fire alarm off the ceiling with a broom handle just because I couldn't reach the button to turn it off quickly enough.

It's embarrassing to admit that my temper snaps at such ridiculous things. I'm ashamed, actually. But my fear is not that I'll have to replace yet another smoke detector; it's that I'll lose my patience at something much more difficult to replace or repair. What keeps me from snapping at my dog when she barks, or at my sons when they don't stop whining? And what damage could I cause if I didn't keep control?

Perhaps that's why God is having me write a chapter on self-control, huh?

Self-control and self-discipline are actually common topics in the Bible. It's quite clear that we are supposed to take responsibility for our behavior and attitude. Proverbs is packed with warnings about what lack of self-control looks like. Proverbs 25:28 and 13:3 can be combined into that old war phrase, "Loose lips sink ships." But my favorite is Proverbs 11:22, which compares a loose woman to jewelry on a pig: in other words, she is a complete waste of something otherwise valuable.

Smashing inanimate objects in a fit of rage or making snide, sarcastic comments about people does not enhance my appearance at all. In fact, lack of self-control is a very ugly trait indeed. No amount of lipstick is going to make that pig look pretty.

So why do I have to deal with situations that push my buttons anyway? If God wants me to be perfect, then why do my flaws flash like DayGlo under a black light? What's the purpose of that?

> For thou, O God, hast proved us: thou hast tried
> us, as silver is tried.
> —*Psalm 66:10*

Do you know how silver is refined? There are several successful ways to refine silver, but all of them involve extreme heat. Being refined is often an unpleasant experience. In Psalm 66, David writes about the refining process Israel had gone through in Egypt. Being enslaved and subjected as a people had driven them together and cemented their identity as the Nation of God. Throughout the Old Testament, every time Israel was driven into exile its people returned purified to a greater degree. It is interesting to note, however, that there were several cycles of exile before Israel finally gave up idolatry for good. So don't expect to excise all your bad habits at once. By the same token, neither should I expect I won't need to continually work on my weaknesses.

Happily, none of us have to work alone! God, through Jesus, has given us the Holy Spirit. This Spirit is the mysterious third part of the Trinity, God Himself in us who have received salvation. Titus 2:11-14 explains how the Spirit works. What a relief! I have the grace of God on my side if I'll just slow down long enough to listen. The Spirit empowers us to say "no" ... but only those who submit to the Teacher are going to learn anything. Just like we know we'll get a failing grade if we never do the homework, we should know that being taught by God is a cooperative experience.

For me, that means if I'm going to get my temper and my tongue under control, I need to pry my sleepy self out of bed every morning before everyone else and dedicate a quiet 30 minutes to God. I have learned over the years that I need structure, so I find and follow a devotional program. Then I ponder and pray about what I've read and what's going on in my life in my journal. I've learned I need to write out my prayers. Writing forces me to focus and to be more honest with myself and with God.

One friend finds she prays best while walking. Keeping her body busy allows her mind to focus on what she's praying about. Another friend prays on her knees. The point is not about process. I don't care how you pray or in what order you read your Bible; the point is that you do it.

It is during those quiet times that I can usually think objectively about the situations that set me off, asking God what I should be doing as opposed to what I have been doing. And it is during those quiet times that the Lord reminds me I have already been given the gifts I need to handle a life more like God designed.

I am pleased to report that God is faithful. I have been refined and am a better reflector of my Heavenly Father than I was before. But I'm a long way from a perfect mirror of my Lord. So I submit to further refining, and anticipate that God will continue to heat, purify, cool and polish me for the rest of my life.

If anything, life with Christ is never boring—at least not if you're paying attention!

Chapter Worksheet

Suggested Group Activity

Ask group members to name an item of food they find irresistible; ask them to describe what it tastes like. Remind them that this should go quickly, with each person sharing briefly. Then say, "It's interesting that what is difficult for one person to resist might not be for another—much like life."

Ask each person to write down one thing or one area of life in which he or she needs to develop or exercise more self-control. Challenge group members to spend time each day, for one week, praying about this and developing a strategy for improvement.

Going Deeper
Bible Study

What sets you off? Do certain noises push your buttons, like they do me? Or does the scent of chocolate turn you into an unstoppable eating machine? (Yeah, I fight that one too.) What about other temptations: talking too much, physical intimacy with the wrong people, headstrong self-determination? The list of options is quite long and very personal.

Let's look at someone who had a laundry list of control issues; maybe we can draw some parallels.

> The woman gave birth to a boy and named him
> Samson. He grew and the Lord blessed him,
> and the Spirit of the Lord began to stir him
> while he was in Mahaneh Dan, between Zorah
> and Eshtaol.
>
> —*Judges 13:24-25*

(Note: The Hebrew behind *to stir him* means "to thrust, impel, push, beat persistently.")

According to my Bible study notes, Samson was from the tribe of Dan, which still had not completely conquered its inherited lands after 300 years—but that is a whole series of other stories. The Philistines hadn't gotten the eviction notice, so the Israelites weren't settled and were nomads in their own country. Mahaneh Dan was the battle camp of the tribe; it was there that God stirred up in Samson the warlike energy and leadership skills that would make him memorable.

I find it fascinating that Samson felt God's direction so strongly. However, this does not mean Samson always did everything right.

Read Judges 14:1-7. Do you think it might have been difficult for Samson to defy his parents' concerned advice? After all, marrying the enemy is bad enough, but it was doubly wrong for a dedicated Nazirite.

Read Judges 14:8-9.

Read Judges 14:10-14.

Now things get soap opera ugly.

Read Judges 14:15-15:17. Note, in turn, what the characters do in the order they are mentioned:

1. The groomsmen
2. The bride
3. She
4. The men
5. Samson
6. The bride
7. Samson
8. The Philistines
9. Samson
10. The Philistines
11. Samson
12. The Israelites

So, now Samson tops the Philistines' Most Wanted list.

Read Judges 16:1-3. Samson must have been physically huge, because he removes the city gates on his own. However, "the Lord came on him" is conspicuously absent for the rest of Samson's life.

The question is: Who moved?

Read Judges 16:4-19. How many times did it take before Delilah wore down Samson? How long did the bride cry? What does this tell us about Samson?

Read Judges 16:20. Was it really about the hair?

Read Judges 16:21-31. When the hair on Samson's head began to grow again, what else may have been returning?

Read Judges 16:28. This is the first time we hear Samson pray. What does he ask for?

How would your struggles be different if you remembered to pray each time you struggled? What if prayer became a habit?

Questions for Group Discussion

- How would you rate yourself on the 'self-control' scale of 1-10 and why?

- What motivates you to change?

- What social problems (both nationally and worldwide) result from people "out of control?"

- How does the power of the Holy Spirit work to redeem human failure?

- Tell of an experience of God's transforming spirit at work in your life or in the world.

CHAPTER 7

Bizarrely Moral for a Vampire

LIKE MOST FATHERS, CHARLIE is intensely protective of Bella, even though he is largely clueless about teenage girls as a whole. In the second novel, *Eclipse*, Charlie finally works up the courage to have "the talk" with Bella. She tries to explain how old-fashioned Edward is, but Charlie doesn't believe it until she blurts out the fact that she's still a virgin.

A lot has been said about the morality Edward displays by refusing to have sex with Bella. Critics of the series say the whole reason he doesn't have sex is so he won't kill her—plain and simple—and that morality has nothing to do with it. Supporters of the series are enamored with the old-fashioned value of purity that Edward seems to yearn to preserve. I fall in with the second group, since Edward does say that sexual purity before marriage is one point they have in common and one Commandment he has not broken.

Why is it so hard for Bella to accept his "no, not yet?" Why is it hard to abstain, not only from illicit sex but also from other behavior that is unhealthy, harmful or corrupt? Why is it so hard for us to accept "not yet" from God?

It's hard to wrap our heads around just how different the world was 100 years ago. Even 50 years ago, for that matter. When I was in college, an adult student told me how completely unacceptable it was for those in her generation to have sex before marriage, no matter what someone's religious background or belief. Sex was for marriage, period. It was scandalous when word got out that a girl had "lost" her virginity. It was something to be ashamed of.

I think that began to change about 50 years ago. The 1960s ushered in the sexual revolution and young adults began to throw off the morals taught by previous generations. Thirty years ago, that generation began raising its own children—many of whom were born into a perfect storm of moral decay.

The "Love Generation" couldn't—or wouldn't—condemn behavior in its children that parents had experienced themselves. All sorts of things became acceptable and "normal" that had been taboo or unusual for teens—or, at least, hushed for adults—of the previous generation. Compounding the problem, the birth of MTV and a culture of youth consumerism brought about an increasingly rapid normalization of immoral behavior.

In 1988, when I graduated from high school, it was as common to have had sex before graduation as it was to have remained a virgin. By 2002, statistics reported 65-70 percent of 18-year-olds as being sexually active. This culture puts enormous pressure on teens. Parents: your kids are seriously living in a different world.

More drastic than participation, though, is the change of attitude. "Back in the day," when I was in high school, sexual activity was something you didn't talk about much. However, the effects of the attitudes seen in *Brat Pack* movies quickly set in. Fifteen years later I was back in a high school classroom as an adult, where I observed students talking about sexual activity as if it were a badge of honor.

Not only has the level of sexual activity increased over the years, but the shame that kept a damper on that activity has been replaced with a dangerous sense of entitlement and pride. The societal pressure is exactly the opposite of what it was just 50 years ago. Now it's the kid who has no sexual experience who is shamed.

So, yes, the world is a different place for Bella than it was for Edward. But should that really make a difference if we're talking about personal purity? Of course not. God is timeless and so are ethics; the morals of the current era or culture are immaterial. Even today, what is morally acceptable behavior differs in various cultures around the world.

> **God is timeless and so are ethics; the morals of the current era or culture are immaterial.**

Living a life of purity is not so different from living the life of a vampire: there's only one rule. For a Christian, every rule, guideline, Commandment, restriction and allowance hangs on just one hook: *God first.*

It's not that God doesn't want you to have sex. Like all good things, sex was God's idea first, you know. What do you think God meant when he said Adam and Eve would become "one flesh" in Genesis

2:22-24? There's a euphemism for intercourse if I ever heard one!

While God also told Adam and Eve to "be fruitful and increase in number" (Genesis 1:28), sex is about much more than procreation; otherwise, the teen pregnancy rate would either be phenomenally higher than it is now or all these abstinence programs would be redundant. Scripture tells us that it is good for a man and woman to leave their parents to be joined together as one flesh, united in marriage.

But a warning: if you get it out of order—sex before commitment—you risk distorting God's best plan for your life and bringing upon your own head the weight of regret and pain He's been trying to save you from.

I am not naïve. I will not assume you've never had sex. If you are a virgin, preserve that gift. View your sexuality as a gift from God: something precious to be valued, worthy of tenderness and respect. But I did not. I had to swallow my pride and confess to the man who would become my husband that I was not a virgin. I was so ashamed and so sorry that I hadn't waited for this good man, so I could have given him my best.

For those who are in the boat I was in, there is grace. God is so good to us! Even though we sometimes ignore or abandon God's plan for us and do what we want instead, God is ready to forgive us the moment we ask. Paul writes to a group of new believers in Corinth, to help them understand just what forgiveness means. Look up 1 Corinthians 6:9-11 and take note of the wide variety of backgrounds that God had forgiven and called to a higher life. Of course there were the usual: the greedy, the drunks, the gossips and the cheaters; but Paul also included sexual sins as well: single people who had had sex before marriage, adulterers and, just in case anyone had any questions, he included prostitutes. That's a pretty comprehensive list, yeah? And the standards are quite clear. At the risk of upsetting my hairdresser and a few relatives, I don't care whom you're sleeping with: if the person you're sleeping with is not your married partner, it is sin.

Argue with Paul if you will, but for Jesus, Genesis was authority enough. He quotes it in Matthew 19:4-6 when explaining why divorce is such a bad thing. This scripture focuses especially on the permanence of the physical connection between husband and wife. Intercourse is described as becoming one flesh. Of course, at this there was a whole lot of "But, but, but, what about ..." arguments, to which Jesus countered that although Moses allowed divorce, God doesn't—unless one partner is unfaithful. At that, the disciples—sarcastic lot that they were—said that maybe no one should get married if divorce is such a difficult thing to obtain. And Jesus, surprisingly, said "Maybe not ..." Those are red-letter words! You might not agree with Paul, but the ice gets awfully thin when you start shaking off Jesus' advice.

Some have chosen to focus on serving God rather than on pursuing a marital relationship with the opposite sex; they have chosen celibacy. Persons in these situations are not holding out for a human partner, but are preserving themselves and their energies for God Himself.

Divorce is always painful. There are no time limits on how long those involved suffer. Perhaps the high divorce rates should be warning signals for those who rush into relationships. In the *Twilight* series, Bella seems to have difficulty being alone. She only feels secure when she is in a relationship with a man. When Edward leaves her in the second book of the series, she quickly attaches herself to Jacob Black. She only feels whole when she is close to a male friend. As Christians, we should be most aware that the only "person" Who can truly fulfill us is the Spirit of God through Jesus Christ. No other human being can totally fulfill the emptiness in our hearts and that deep longing to be connected.

That is a place reserved for God. When we submit ourselves first to God and allow this transforming Spirit to make us whole, only then are we prepared to be in relationships with others.

When we are deceived by the feelings of "love"—the thrill of a new relationship and the possibility of finding the one and only best love of our lives—we may enter into sexual relations hastily, without careful and prayerful consideration. If we fall victim to peer pressure to "just get it over with" (referring to losing our virginity), we lose something precious that comes from two becoming one. Sex and intercourse should be more than a physical act. I heard a popular Christian evangelist and sociologist say that the average person "falls in love" seven times before he is married ... and seven times after he is married! Marriage is a commitment of the heart and the will to remain faithful, sexually, to each other.

Sex is a wonderful gift when shared with someone we have committed ourselves to, with promises to love and cherish ... until death do us part. It is not to be entered into lightly or casually. A healthy marriage is one in which two people nurture and support each other. Jesus used marriage as the picture of His relationship with the Church, calling the Church the "bride of Christ." It is interesting to note that in the *Twilight* series, Bella and Edward's marriage is one for eternity and with no time limits. The author of *Twilight* is a Mormon; this concept of eternal marriage reflects her Mormon belief system.

Bella would suffer a lot less internal conflict if she would accept the simple concept that she is, as you are, worth waiting for. Perhaps she would also have less internal conflict if she fully understood and experienced the unconditional love of God through Jesus Christ. She certainly would be less needy, less boy crazy and more stable in all of her relationships.

I know this is not going to be a popular or easy-to-swallow chapter. It flies in the face of every media message that constantly bombards us.

Chapter Worksheet

Suggested Group Activity

Have the group brainstorm all the words and phrases used for sexual intercourse. These are not necessarily the words they might use, but the list should include everything they have ever heard. Write these down on a large sheet of newsprint so that everyone can see.

This is meant to be a serious activity to help understand our feelings and attitudes toward "two becoming one."

After you have a fairly complete list, ask the group to identify which words or phrases make sexual intercourse sound like (some will fall into one or more categories):

1. A game or athletic activity—put a * mark beside each word or phrase

2. Something dirty, lewd, vulgar or course—put a line through each word or phrase

3. A position of power, control or status—put a > mark beside it

4. Something shameful, bad or guilt-inducing—put an X mark on it

5. A violent, forceful, brutal or sadistic act—put two lines through each word or phrase

6. Something insignificant, trivial or silly—put a @ mark beside it

7. Work, a duty or drudgery—put a smiley face beside it

8. Something loving, tender, nurturing and caring—put a circle and star!

- What do you discern from this activity?

- How do the words we use to describe the act of sex reflect our attitudes toward sex?

- How are our attitudes toward sexuality formed?

Questions for Group Discussion

- What is healthy or good about Bella's relationship with Edward? What is unhealthy or immature about the relationship?

- At the beginning of the chapter, the author discusses how times have changed regarding attitudes toward sex. What has your experience been? Describe ways media and culture effect our attitudes toward sexuality.

- In the Old Testament, polygamy was common, yet today most in a Western society would deplore the practice. Many tribes around the world still find polygamy acceptable. How does one determine what is right and what is wrong regarding marriage and sexual relationships?

- How have various interpretations of Scripture influenced ethics involving marriage, divorce and sex?

- One area of great pain and disagreement within and outside of various denominations is homosexuality and gender issues. If you have established trust in your group, you may want to prayerfully discuss your feelings, experiences and views.

- What are your own struggles concerning fidelity of sexuality within marriage?

CHAPTER 8

Sacrificial Pire

AT THE END OF *Breaking Dawn,* we learn that Bella and Edward's child, Renesmee, is not unique: she is not the only half-human/half-vampire being to have been born. We do learn, however, that Bella is unique for having survived the experience. Even then, she did not survive as a human; only the transformation into vampire repaired the damage caused by Renesmee's violent vampire birth.

Shortly after Renesmee's birth, the Cullen family meets Nahuel, a half-human/half-vampire being from South America. From his aunt, they learn the story of his birth; about his mother, Pire; and about her willing sacrifice for her unborn child. While still in the womb, Nahuel became strong enough to break her bones. Pire realized his birth would kill her, yet she loved him and begged her sister to take care of him.

As soon as Bella realized she was pregnant with Edward's child, she became equally unreasonable. It quickly became apparent that this child was destroying her body, but she refused to take any action that would damage the baby—even to save her own life.

Much like Bella through most of the *Twilight* series, I could not imagine myself as a mother. As a child, my baby dolls were much more interesting for what I could put on them than for what I would pretend to feed them. Even after marrying and knowing my husband would be a good father to our children, we became pregnant with our first child and it *still* wasn't real. I still wasn't ready to be "Mommy."

A few months into my first pregnancy, I woke up thinking I might be miscarrying. At that moment, when faced with the possibility of losing my firstborn, I realized how precious being a mother—and the gift of life that goes with it—really is. I woke my husband in a panic and called the doctor at an hour that otherwise should be illegal. God was gracious to me. My precious firstborn son is now in elementary school. Every day he brings me a new joy, even when he's testing the limits of my patience.

Oh, what I wouldn't do for my children! The list is fairly short. I am certain a mother bear would look tame compared to me, if anyone were to threaten my children. But any sacrifice I would make for my children pales in comparison to what my Creator has done for me. For us to attempt to comprehend the scope of God's sacrifice would be to trivialize the enormous significance of this act of love for eternity and for all humankind.

Pire sacrificed her life for Nahuel. Bella was willing to sacrifice her life for her daughter, Renesmee. But I wonder if either of them would sacrifice her life for someone else—for a stranger. Would I? For what or whom are we willing to give up our lives?

Can we begin to comprehend the depths of love expressed through Christ on the cross?

What is the meaning of sacrifice? According to my tattered Webster's Dictionary, sacrifice is: "3a: destruction or surrender of something for the sake of something else."

In Old Testament times, God accepted the sacrifice of animals as atonement for sin. But why was a sacrifice necessary? Sacrifice was essentially the only means of forgiveness and "getting right" with God. It was the way to escape God's wrath. This was integral to the life of the covenant community; of the chosen people of God. They knew no other way. In the New Testament, the people are offered a New Way, through the atonement of Jesus Christ's death and resurrection.

Atonement literally means "to be at one with." It was at great sacrifice that people purchased a sacrificial animal. Recall Joseph and Mary's offering of two doves at the Temple following the birth of their son, Jesus: adherence to the Jewish code often meant a financial sacrifice for those making the offering.

In the creation story, there was no need for atonement and sacrifice because God and humankind were "at one" with each other. Adam and Eve walked daily with God. But as soon as Adam and Eve put their own will and desires before the perfect will of God, they were forced from the Garden (Genesis 3). They sinned.

The result of sin was death. Every sin required atonement. After a few millennia, that's a lot of dead cattle, sheep, goats and doves. Eventually, people began to lose the point. The process became as empty as most New Year's resolutions.

Sacrificial offerings became merely a practice that made people feel better, without actually implementing change in the way they lived. It was no longer a transforming experience from sinfulness to "at-one-ness" with God.

In Isaiah Chapter 1, God expresses grief over the abuse of the sacrificial system, calling the offerings "meaningless." The people were not allowing their hearts to be changed by the process. They had gotten it backwards: God did not desire the blood of sacrifice on the altar as much as He desired a cleansing of their hearts. Those well-known words from this chapter remind us that "tho our sins be scarlet as blood, they will become white as snow" through true repentance and turning from sin.

Verse 17 is especially descriptive, as God outlines what is truly desired: to choose right over wrong, defend the powerless, champion justice and take care of widows and orphans. It doesn't sound that difficult, yet it's easier to buy a bull and slap it on the altar than it is to change a selfish heart.

As you continue to read Isaiah, you quickly learn that a better way is coming—a new form of atonement that will remove animal sacrifice forever. The process of sacrifice merely foreshadowed a better way.

We are justified in God's sight through the atoning work of Christ on the cross.

> The next day John (saw) Jesus coming unto him,
> and (said), 'Behold the Lamb of God, which
> (takes) away the sin of the world.'
> —*John 1:29*

The Bible has been called the History of Salvation. God's gift of salvation is often viewed primarily as deliverance from eternal punishment, but it also includes a transformation of life itself. From early times, theologians have debated and analyzed the doctrines of salvation and atonement. Perhaps that is why various denominations and sects can never agree completely on their meanings. An early concept in church history is that of *blood ransom*.

The verses in John foretell a time when, instead of hundreds of thousands of sheep being slaughtered for the sins of humanity, one sheep—the most pure of lambs—would die a horrible death to remove every sin once and for all. What is shattering to me is the realization that Jesus would still die if I were the only one in history who had sinned. My sins alone justified this sacrifice. More astounding still, His sacrifice alone justifies everyone who accepts it.

Back to the question: What if I was called upon to sacrifice myself to save my son? How would I feel? Terrified, I imagine. What if it wasn't my son I was throwing myself in front of a car for, but someone I'd never met? Even more difficult to answer is this: What cause is great enough that I would sacrifice my son?

Anselm of Canterbury suggested that only God could atone for humanity's sin, as nothing else would be great enough. There is nothing above God. God is entitled to righteousness; sin is not part of God's nature. To address the injustice of sin required a worthy sacrifice: the atonement of the people through the death of Jesus. Anselm offers that Christ alone could mediate between God and humankind.

I often wonder what Jesus felt as he faced death on the cross. Those paintings of Jesus in the Garden of Gethsemane depict Him serenely kneeling at a rock with the halo of light around His head. Not like that, it turns out ...

> And He was withdrawn from them about a
> stone's cast, and kneeled down, and prayed.
> —*Luke 22:41*

Originally written in Greek, the words behind this verse are much more graphic than the polite picture we get here.

Jesus tore Himself away from his friends. He was reluctant to be alone. He did not lower himself slowly to his knees; He dropped suddenly. He fell flat. He collapsed on the ground to pray those classic words, "not My will, but Yours be done."

> And being in an agony He prayed more earnestly: and His sweat was as it were great drops of blood falling down to the ground.
>
> —*Luke 22:44*

Remember in *Breaking Dawn* when Renesmee is born and the capillaries in Bella's eyes pop, becoming instantly bloodshot? Under extreme stress, the capillaries under the skin will also pop, causing blood to seep out of the skin. The stress and fear Jesus felt—the weight of the burden He was carrying to the sacrificial altar—was so great, He literally sweat blood. The word *anguish* translated is *agōnia*, the obvious root of the English word *agony*. It also means "to struggle for victory." Jesus, the Divine Son, the Lamb of God sent to take away the sin of the world, struggled with His mission and asked God for a way out if any other way could be found. It is reassuring to realize that even Jesus struggled.

Atonement is beyond us and our capabilities. It is the gift of God through Jesus Christ. The enormity of His sacrifice is described vividly in the great hymn of the Christian Church, *O Sacred Head Now Wounded*. The second verse reads:

> What Thou, my Lord has suffered was all for
> sinners' gain;
> Mine, mine was the transgression,
> but Thine the deadly pain.
> Lo, here I fall, my Savior!
> 'Tis I deserve thy place;
> look on me with Thy favor,
> vouchsafe to me thy grace.
>
> —*Anonymous, Middle Ages*

There was God the Father, watching the Son suffering; dying for all of humanity. Can we begin to comprehend the depths of love expressed through Christ on the cross?

Every day and in a million ways we are beset by messages that feed our insecurities, but all the while God whispers, "Look to the cross. Listen to Me. Respond to My love. You are worth it."

You are worth Jesus' sacrifice. Jesus died so you can be in God's presence not just in Heaven but now, here, in this life. That sacrifice—that atonement—offers you a life so connected with God that, like Adam and Eve in the Garden, you can walk and talk with God all the time, all day long and every day for the rest of your life. All you need to do is accept the gift.

Receive, and believe in, an atonement that will take away the shame of your past and shed hopeful light into your future. What could possibly be better than that? Honestly, nothing. You have been given God's love. Open your heart and embrace it.

Chapter Worksheet

Suggested Group Activity

Pass out index cards to the group. Ask members to write brief summaries of examples of people expressing sacrificial love. Write only one case on each card. For example: An elderly spouse who devotes his or her life to caring for an ailing partner. Do not give personal details or names. Collect the completed cards. Shuffle them and redistribute the cards equally among participants. Each person takes a turn reading their card's contents aloud to the group.

Follow this activity with a prayer of thanksgiving for those willing to express sacrificial love. Pray for these people and for those gathered, that people of faith might act out this type of love in God's world.

Going Deeper
Bible Study

- When you read about Jesus' struggle in the Garden of Gethsemane, what is your reaction?

- How do you interpret the pain that God the Father suffered when He offered His Son as a sacrifice?

- Is it easy for you to dismiss your interpretation and just walk away, unchanged? Or are you compelled to change with your realization?

- In what ways do we live out the profound gift of God's sacrificial love?

- Read Romans 12:1-2.

- In light of God's gift, is being a "living sacrifice" a hard thing to do?

- The King James Version of verse 1 offers a more practical interpretation; one that is more difficult to think your way out of:

> I beseech you therefore, brethren, by the mercies of God, that ye present your bodies a living sacrifice, holy, acceptable unto God, [which is] your reasonable service.

Reasonable. Spiritual act of worship is a little hard to grasp, but *reasonable?* Well, it's so reasonable.

A Biblical Reality Check

- How are we transformed?

- How are our minds renewed?

- Once we put this into practice, what is the reward (Romans 12:2)?

- And who, really, wouldn't want that?

Questions for Group Discussion

- What is the most sacrificial gift you've ever received?

- What is the most sacrificial gift you ever gave?

- Which of the above experiences was easier—and why?

- What is your understanding of atonement?

- What is your experience with atonement?

CHAPTER 9

He's Gone

IN *NEW MOON*, **EDWARD** endeavors to do the right thing. Edward wants Bella to remain human. He also wants to remove the dangers and temptations of being around vampires from her life. So he breaks up with her and moves away. His entire vampire family moves from Forks. His fervent desire, even though it breaks his heart, is that she will get over him. He wants her to live out her life as a normal person. His hope is that time will heal her broken heart.

It doesn't work. Bella walks around feeling hollow, like her heart has been ripped out—along with other vital organs. She functions out of a sense of duty to her father and her friends. She tries to keep up a brave face so her father won't worry too much. Months pass, but the wound does not heal. She continues to ache. Nightmares visit her every night.

She is beyond heartbroken; she is completely shattered.

No one escapes heartbreak. But what do you do when you feel like there is nothing worth living for?

Prince's *1999* was on every radio station that night. It was December 31, 1999; the eve of a new millennium. The celebration worldwide was epic. All afternoon I had been watching the festivities creep around the globe as I was personally counting down to a date I'd been anticipating. I was 29 and single. I looked forward to testing the premise that whomever you kiss at midnight on New Year's Eve is the person with whom you spend the coming year.

After waiting a reasonable amount of time past when we were to meet, I waited some more. I waited twice as long as was sane but still, I waited. Looking back, I waited an irrationally long time.

I had traveled so far to get to that night, both physically and emotionally. Years earlier I had given up my own will and submitted my dating life to God. I thought this man was the answer; a reward for my obedience. I had driven hours from my home and was staying at my parents' so I could be with him for this once-in-a-lifetime, turn-of-the-century event.

All of the hopes I had pinned on those few hours didn't go down in a blaze of glory. They didn't explode. They were more measured and laboriously painful than that. The experience was much darker. It felt like a chemical burn that corroded me from the inside out. It only got worse as the hours passed. When I finally gave up and returned to my parents' house, I was relieved to find they were still at church. I couldn't talk. I wasn't up to an explanation. I had no explanation to give anyway. I crawled into the small, cold guest bed in the basement, turned my face to the wall and cried.

Months later, my friends—the pastor and his wife, whom I worked with as a youth minister—said they thought I wasn't going to make it. They had been afraid I might quit and move home because of the pain. That surprised me; I thought I'd sucked it up and soldiered on pretty well.

The hollowness left behind by a lost love—or the lost hope of love—is undeniable. It is deep, fierce and relentless. For some reason this experience seemed worse than any broken heart I'd experienced before. This time, the pain seemed pure and somehow innocent. It was unsullied by the guilt of a relationship gone too far and therefore tempered by the impression that I somehow deserved the pain.

Bella, after months of trying not to feel, became an adrenaline junkie. She attempted to force hallucinations into her reality. She began to search for ways to fill the void and numb the pain. Over and over Bella refers to the hole in her heart and instinctively holds her chest in an attempt to keep from falling apart even more.

How different is she from us, when we try to fill that unnamed, indefinable hole inside ourselves with relationships, activities or addictions? Do I need to say it? Do I need to point out that, from birth, we are born with an aching void that we spend our lives trying to fill? As St. Augustine once said, "You have made us for Yourself, O Lord, and our hearts are restless until they rest in You."

Why *wouldn't* it hurt all the way to the deepest, most undefined edges, when those silly, inadequate little patches are torn off and our entire ache for God is once again revealed?

So many people walk through life unaware of that hole. I would say "blissfully," but that's not true. Some search for an "Edward" or "Bella" of their own. Some search for power and recognition. Sometimes addiction is the result of our attempts to numb the pain. Even healthy endeavors, such as running or exercise, can become excessive. Each is a manifestation of that vacuum. Any bliss captured during those searches is temporary and empty.

In the months following Mother Teresa's death, the world was surprised to learn this venerable saint of service had a secret she kept close to the vest: Mother Teresa confided in a very few trusted priests that she had not heard from God in decades. For years she had lived faithfully in the dark night of the soul. The news sent shockwaves through the world; how could such a woman, obviously called and empowered by God, feel so remote from God's presence?

I have thought of four reasons why one might find herself suffering such darkness:

1. You have walked away from God through choice. Perhaps you experienced a crisis or an event that challenged your faith and, rather than go deeper, you gave up and walked the opposite way.

Hosea Chapter 5 graphically describes what happens when we exile ourselves from God. In God's eyes, we whore ourselves out, blinding ourselves and stumbling around in the dark—all needlessly—when we refuse to turn from our sins and seek Him first. When we walk away from God through choice, our gracious God waits patiently for us to return.

> I will go [and] return to my place, till they
> acknowledge their offence, and seek My face: in
> their affliction they will seek Me early.
> —*Hosea 5:15*

When you examine yourself in light of the scriptures, have you intentionally walked away from God? You *can* come home; just recommit and seek His strength.

2. This could be a time of testing. In Matthew, Jesus was tempted in the desert, weak and alone, with the three great questions:

- Are you physically disciplined? In Matthew 4:1-4, Jesus had been fasting for 40 days and nights—so of course he was hungry. Would you have the discipline to abstain from eating when given the opportunity to eat your fill?

- Are you spiritually trusting? In Matthew 4:5-7, the Tempter quotes the Bible to Jesus, daring Him to test God about something He already knows. Are you asking God to answer an unnecessary question—one that has already been answered for you?

- Are you socially humble? Matthew 4:8-10 begs the question: What if Jesus did not have God at the center of His purpose in life? Would He have used His charisma, His intellect or His driving passions to rule the world? We are typically not asked questions that do not tempt us. Can you relate to the desire for power and popularity? How do you respond in social situations?

3. It is time for you to take off the training wheels and walk in the wisdom and strength you have gained in God's presence. Jesus warns us that moving in God-given authority brings us into the firing line of the enemy. That does not excuse us from the battle. We are to take courage from the promise that God, through the Holy Spirit, will provide for all of our needs.

> But beware of men: for they will deliver you up to the councils, and they will scourge you in their synagogues; And ye shall be brought before governors and kings for my sake, for a testimony against them and the Gentiles. But when they deliver you up, take no thought how or what ye shall speak: for it shall be given you in that same hour what ye shall speak. For it is not ye that speak, but the Spirit of your Father which speaketh in you.

4. You are so in love with God and He with you that—similar to Edward with Bella—there must be distance so that you can accomplish the tasks set before you. I believe this is why Jesus was called out of the desert after the temptation by news of John's imprisonment; otherwise, He may have rested with the angels much longer (Matthew 4:11-17).

I also believe that this was Mother Teresa's situation. She was so ecstatically in love with Christ that she would have chosen worship over action if given the choice—but her work and ours is so vital that God graciously removed the choice.

In my darkness, I had a comfort Bella did not. She tried to fill that inborn, God-shaped hole with the god-like Edward, and felt the emptiness even more clearly with Edward's absence. I had filled it by the only One who fits, before I ever met the man who abandoned me that New Year's Eve. In the deepest darkness of that New Year's morning, I cried to God. While some of the questions I had that night have never been answered, I was never truly alone. My recovery has been more than complete.

Chapter Worksheet

Suggested Group Activity

Pass out several slips of paper to each person. Ask every-one to write one word or phrase on each piece of paper, describing how it feels to be abandoned. Collect them. Ask one person to read the words out loud and another to write them on a large piece of newsprint—putting a check mark beside a word if it is used more than once.

Going Deeper
Bible Study

In this chapter the author offered four possible reasons you might feel a God gap in your life. Choose the one you most relate to (or add your own):

1. You have walked away from God by choice. Examine yourself in light of Scripture. Are you honoring God in every area of your life? If not, recommit and seek His strength. Read Hosea 5:4-7, 15 as a group.

2. This is a time of testing. In Matthew 4:1-10, Jesus was tempted in the desert. Weak and alone, he was presented with three questions: Are you physically disciplined? Are you spiritually trusting? Are you socially humble? Read Matthew 4:1-10 as a group.

3. It is time for you to take off the training wheels and walk in the wisdom and strength you have gained. Jesus warns us that moving in the authority of God brings us into the firing line of the enemy. Read Matthew 10:17-20 as a group.

4. You are so in love with God, and He with you, that He must distance His presence from you so that you may accomplish the tasks He has set before you. I believe this is why Jesus was called out of the desert by news of John's death. I also believe that this was Mother Teresa's situation. She was so ecstatically in love with Christ that she would have chosen worship over action if given the choice—but her work was (and ours is) so vital that God graciously removed the choice. Read Matthew 4:11-17 as a group.

In all four circumstances, the absence of God is an opportunity for growth.

Ponder these questions:

• What do you do when you find another caught in a similar vacuum?

• When are you judgmental about someone else's faith journey?

• How are your eyes open to helping those who need light on the way?

Questions for Group Discussion

- Recall a time or situation in your life when you felt abandoned by another person.

- Recall a time or situation in your life when you felt abandoned or separated from God.

- What filled the emptiness?

- What did you learn through these experiences? How have they shaped you?

- How did these experiences help you grow in faith?

CHAPTER 10

A "Vegetarian" Diet

WHEN WE FIRST REALLY get to know Jasper in *Eclipse,* he tells us how easy it was to walk away from his first vampire friends. Their relationship was one of convenience. It was a partnership that allowed them to do whatever they wanted when they wanted; to kill and feed whenever they desired.

In *Breaking Dawn,* a new character is introduced: Eleazar, a friend of the Cullen family. Eleazar is from another vampire family that also feeds on animals rather than people. He believes that the true bonds of love come from the civilized practice of abstaining from human blood.

The practice of denying themselves something they wanted but didn't need gave the "vegetarian" vampires a surprising gift: the ability to live together in families. God calls us to deny ourselves also, through fasting and spiritual disciplines. Through these disciplines we, too, are given the gift of living in the family of God. The results can literally be miraculous.

The date is 605 B.C.E. It's been approximately 1,500 years since God promised Abraham that his children would become God's chosen people. Approximately 1,000 years have passed since Jacob, Abraham's grandson, prophesied that Judah, Jacob's son, would be the father of many kings. It has been 500 years since that prophesy was realized through the appointment of David as King of Israel.

In 1,000 years, Israel grew from a single nomadic tribe consisting of Abraham, his wife and a nephew to a mighty nation. The story is dramatic and inspiring. The following 500-year death spiral was a warning to proud nations and individuals alike: decades of self-indulgent leadership, an absent covenant community that left society without a moral compass and folks happy to follow the governments' collapsing standards (wow, doesn't that sound familiar) resulted in Israel being overrun by its surrounding nations. Most of the citizenry were carted off into slavery by the superpower of the day, King Nebuchadnezzar of Babylon (Daniel 1:1-5).

It had been 500 years since David was crowned king. Considering the fact that most kings had wives and concubines in abundance, there had to have been an excess of cousins with royal lineage. From that group, King Nebuchadnezzar suggested the chief of his court pick the best and brightest to be taught Babylonian history, literature and language over the course of the next three years. If the "chosen ones" did well, these young Israelites would get to serve in their new king's court; if not, they might not be holding their breath inside their bodies much longer. Perhaps as a reward—or as a way to help the captives feel attached to their Babylonian ruler—the pupils would be fed food from Nebuchadnezzar's table.

That plan sounded just fine to most of the Israelites. Most knew the king's food and wine was first offered to idols, and that eating it was a form of worshiping a false god. Maybe they took the destruction of their homeland as proof enough that God didn't exist, rather than as testimony that God would not put up with willful disobedience forever. Perhaps their families had become so deeply involved in idol worship at home that this was nothing new; maybe it didn't even cross their minds that this plan might be something risky to their very souls.

> **That plan sounded just fine to most of the Israelites. Maybe they took the destruction of their homeland as proof enough that God didn't exist, rather than as testimony that God would not put up with willful disobedience forever.**

Remember: one vital aspect of Israelite national identity was the Jewish code of dietary restrictions. Outlined to Moses by God during the Exodus, the strict Jewish diet was unparalleled in the ancient world. For example, cattle were considered "clean" because they chew cud and have a split hoof. However, the pig and rabbit were "unclean" because they don't meet those requirements: the pig does not chew cud and the rabbit does not have a split hoof. In fact, Israelites were not even allowed to touch the carcasses of animals that did not meet the Jewish code (Leviticus 11:3-8). There were restrictions on seafood and fowl as well. As you can imagine, being forbidden to eat pork might create some issues when your host is a king who eats pork regularly.

To most of the young men chosen for this "internship," this opportunity was a dream come true: no more war, life in a royal palace, instant prestige and job security for life. What wasn't there to like, if these were the most important things to most Israelites? But Daniel, Hananiah, Mishael and Azariah were not so easily swayed. Perhaps they'd paid more attention in Hebrew school; possibly they were just more homesick than their colleagues and less willing to give up their traditions. Maybe. But one doesn't risk one's life for homesickness, as a general rule.

Astonishingly, these four young captives had the unmitigated gall to suggest they be exempted from the "honor" of eating the king's food. Hananaiah, Mishael and Azariah followed Daniel's lead when he decided he wouldn't play it safe at the expense of his faith. They approached the guy in charge of their education and welfare to ask for an exemption (Daniel 1:6-8).

Somehow, these four preserved their faith and religious teaching in a society that had almost completely turned its back on this ancient wisdom. Now, because of other people's choices, these four good kids were in a horrible situation. They faced a tougher test of character than most people ever will.

The official was hesitant, worrying about his own neck as much as his job security if these guys wasted away to nothing. At the very least, he needed to make sure they were as well taken care of as the horses in Nebuchadnezzar's stable. So Daniel offered the official a compromise: let them eat vegetables and drink water for the next 10 days, and if they were still as healthy as the other young men after their fast, than the official would allow their diet to continue (Daniel 1:10-14).

The definition of *fasting* in the dictionary is to "abstain from food" or to "eat sparingly or abstain from some foods." What Webster's Collegiate doesn't tell us is why Daniel and company would go vegetarian when, before they were captured, they likely had animal protein at every meal. However, my grandfather's ancient Bible dictionary sheds more light on the layers of these young men's motivation: fasting was a public sign of grief and repentance, especially during times of national trouble. Our heroes were remembering their history lessons and the times when Israelites took the hint, humbled themselves and prayed and fasted to find God's will.

To recap and apply: Daniel, Hananiah, Mishael and Azariah are fasting for three reasons:

1. The food is likely idol fodder and they don't want to participate in idol worship. This is not usually a relevant concern in Western society—although the idol of convenience does destroy the health of many, many people each year. Just sayin'. Also, our contemporary culture is plagued by eating disorders. What idolized perceptions of beauty do we worship today?

2. Much of the food available is "unclean." The dietary restrictions placed on the Israelites were stringent— and in scientific hindsight, brilliant. In fact, Jordan Ruben has changed lives by introducing people to a traditional Jewish diet.

3. It is an act of spiritual worship and discipline. Fasting is a physical practice with spiritual significance. Occasionally, fasting seems to move God's hand on our behalf. More often, however, fasting moves us closer to God and more able to receive direction and blessing.

So, to recap, our four guys have spent a week and a half eating split pea soup (obviously without ham) and drinking tap water. When the guard comes in he expects to find them listlessly lying around, ready to tear into the first hunk of red meat offered. But, no! They look better than their counterparts on the king's diet. So the official kept his word. The four friends were no longer even offered the king's food (Daniel 1:15-16).

For me, that would be enough. I would be content to know that God made them healthy just because they made the tough and correct choice. But God is so much cooler than that. Because of their obedience and submission to divine law, God opened the floodgates of Heaven onto these guys. Not only did he give them physical health; he made them super smart too. Daniel was given insight into dreams and visions—something the Babylonians spent a lot of time on. At the end of their three-year AP course, the king himself interviewed all the young men in the program.

> And the king (interviewed) them; and among them all was found none like Daniel, Hananiah, Mishael, and Azariah: therefore stood they before the king. And in all matters of wisdom [and] understanding, that the king enquired of them, he found them 10 times better than all the magicians [and] astrologers that [were] in all his realm.

—*Daniel 1:19-20*

But know: fasting is not an "Old Testament thing." In fact, my Bible mentions several times in *red ink* the value of this spiritual discipline.

In Matthew 6, we learn that we're expected to fast. This is in the middle of a section about a variety of spiritual disciplines, including charity, prayer and stewardship. On each topic, Jesus assumes "when" and not "if." Scripture reads: "When you pray ..." and "When you fast ..." These are considered regular things to do as a part of a healthy spiritual life.

In another passage, Matthew 17:21, Jesus explains to his disciples why they were not able to miraculously cast out a demon. "But this kind does not go out except by prayer and fasting," Jesus told them. Apparently, there are times when fasting is the only way to achieve a necessary goal.

I'm not saying that to be an effective Christian you must be a vegetarian; I *am* saying that in times of difficulty, it is a valuable spiritual practice to fast and pray. The rewards will be amazing, even if they are unexpected. For example: who knew, besides our awesome God, that my prayer and fasting would result in this little book you now hold in your hands?

Chapter Worksheet

Suggested Group Activity

As a group, make a list of the benefits or results of practicing spiritual disciplines. Put a smiley face next to each benefit for the individual and a star beside those of value for the "corporate health" of the body of faith.

Going deeper
Bible Study

When do we fast?

- 2 Samuel 1:12
- Psalm 35:13, Daniel 6:18
- 2 Samuel 12:16
- Esther 4:16
- Acts 13:1-3, 14:21-23

What do we do while fasting?

- Daniel 9:1-4
- 1 Samuel 7:6, Nehemiah 9:1-3
- Deuteronomy 9:18, Nehemiah 9:1
- Jeremiah 36:6

What does God seek through our fasting?

- Ezra 8:21-23
- Isaiah 58:3-9

Is fasting Old Testament only?

- Matthew 6:16-18
- Matthew 9:14-15

Must we always just quit eating?

- Daniel 10:1-3

Questions for Group Discussion

- When have you denied yourself something you wanted but did not need? What was the result and how did you feel?

- Which spiritual disciplines do you find easy to follow and, likewise, which are difficult for you? Why?

- Many faith traditions include the spiritual discipline of fasting. What do you know about fasting in other faith traditions?

- Have you ever considered fasting from an activity other than eating? What did you do and what did you discover through this process?

CHAPTER 11

The World's Best Predator

THERE IS A BALANCE between predator and prey. If predator and prey are not closely matched in strength, the prey can usually count on strength in numbers as a defense strategy. However, this doesn't seem to be an option against the vampires of *Twilight,* who seem to have all the cards.

When Bella tells Edward she's figured out he is a vampire, he tries to explain why it's so dangerous for her to be near him. He is the perfect predator. His appearance is the perfect disguise and bait, but even when those fail, no human can run, hide or escape from his grip.

Sometimes you might feel like evil has had millennia of human history to hone skills to a similar point. It is wise to know your enemy so you can recognize attacks and counter with the weapons that faith has to offer.

The first sermon I remember having heard happened when I was in early elementary school, probably kindergarten or first grade. Pastor Ray Huffman was preaching. The Huffmans were more like grandparents to me than any sort of authoritarian figures. This probably helped make the subject stick in my impressionable mind. I trusted Pastor Huffman completely, and he was completely trustworthy in all the years I knew him.

The text, which I can still find now because I remember so clearly when he read and explained it, is from 1 Peter 5. Pastor Huffman was probably preaching from a larger section about worry and faith, but verse 8 resonated and stuck in my young imagination.

> Be sober, be vigilant; because your adversary the
> devil, as a roaring lion, walketh about, seeking
> whom he may devour.
> *—1 Peter 5:8*

Such an alarming image! Satan as a lion with wide-open jaws, ready to eat me up—until Pastor Huffman pointed out that little word, *like*. It's all a show! Satan has no real lion-like power, because we are defended by the Lion of Judah, he explained. When we are surrounded by the noise and fury of an enemy attack, we can recognize it as such—just a smoke show, cleared away by faith in the only true power in the universe: God Himself.

Satan is one of the world's most potent symbols of evil, from ancient scriptures through Dante, C.S. Lewis and countless Hollywood movies. *Twilight* portrays the timeless "good vs. evil" struggle as the "good" vampires—those who only drink animal blood—fighting the "bad" vampires—those who feast on human blood. In the *Twilight* books, it is fairly easy to sort out who is good from who is bad; in life it is often not so easy. Most of us can probably count on one hand (if we can name any) people who are or were truly evil, totally immoral and depraved without hope of redemption. On the other hand, if we are honest, who is totally good, without sin? Christian teachings point only to one: Jesus Christ. When we fall into the trap of labeling others as either totally good or totally evil, we are headed for trouble and disappointment, often missing opportunities for transformation.

Fortunately, Jesus offers many examples for addressing our natural tendency to stereotype and hold prejudice against a particular group of people. He breaks all sorts of social boundaries when He chooses to offer living water to the Samaritan woman. First of all, Jews did not talk to Samaritans. In fact, most Jews would travel three days out of their way to avoid going through Samaria. Second, men did not talk to women in public. A rabbi most likely would not even address a female relative outside the privacy of home. Yet here is Jesus, talking with a Samaritan woman—in public! This is disgraceful. It would have been considered wrong by all the good, moral Jewish leaders of the day. What is Jesus teaching us about who is good and who is evil? That perhaps we need to be cautious when identifying our enemies. It is dangerous to vilify a particular race, creed or group of persons.

We all have the capacity—a result of free will—to choose good or choose evil. We all have the capacity to do good or to do ill. Paul laments in Romans Chapter 7, verses 15-19, that he finds himself doing that which he would not do; in fact, he says he does what he hates and of the good he wants to do, he fails to do. So we, too, struggle daily to follow Christ, to be continually transformed into the people of God. We struggle with our nature of leaning toward sin and doing what is wrong.

If God is the source of good—the Truth, the Way and the Life—than what is the source of evil?

That image of Satan as a lion and Christ as the Lion of Judah, defending me, was reinforced later by C.S. Lewis and *The Chronicles of Narnia*. The true king of Narnia is Aslan, a lion and the Christ-like figure in the story. I learned more as I read and understood the Bible for myself. What little power evil has is allotted by God for a while, and only to a certain limit. The only true power of evil is deception. Satan is the king of smoke and mirrors.

Satan is a personification of evil. So, who is this Satan figure? Most would agree that Satan is bad and, in fact, quite dangerous. Anyone whose sole purpose in existence is to destroy your soul forever is a threat to be taken seriously. So, then, it would be good to know who our enemy is, and how to completely throw ourselves into the protection of the One Who can defeat him.

Let's start with a story about who Satan was. Ezekiel 28:12-19 contains the history of Satan, as told by God to Ezekiel.

Satan is a creature that truly glitters in the sun, and whose danger goes far beyond just taking human life. Satan started off as one of the highest-ranking angels in God's creation, but over time he began to think that he, the created, could overcome the Creator. Satan's ultimate revenge is to take as many people as he can into Hell with him—the only place God's love and beauty cannot be found.

He is good at it. Satan's pretty much figured out the truth in: "You can catch more flies with honey than vinegar." He is much less likely to pounce like a roaring lion—too obvious—than to ease his way into your life by weaseled invitation. Hence his successful approach to Eve in the Garden was a seemingly innocent question, and not "Eat this fruit or else!" Satan is the ultimate ad man.

In John Chapter 8, Jesus explains Satan's mode of operation when he is arguing with the politically motivated religious leaders of his day. Jesus called the popular preachers and religious lawyers sons of Satan, "who was a murderer from the start, a liar and the father of everyone who lies." Jesus' words delighted a crowd that was tired of being fed mixed messages. His words also seriously offended the power base, which attempted to murder Him on the spot.

Satan's strength is not in overpowering us, but in offering choices that ultimately lead to our self-destruction. He offers the lie that "a little of this won't hurt you," knowing full well that a little bit is all it takes to set the hook. And nothing is more insidious than the smoke-and-mirror suggestion that he doesn't exist at all. But even *that* doesn't hold water.

> **Satan's strength is not in overpowering us, but in offering choices that ultimately lead to our self-destruction.**

In 2 Corinthians 11:14, Satan is called out for disguising himself as an angel of light. He would know how, as his original name, Lucifer, meant *Morning Star*. Verse 3 of the same chapter warns that this is how Eve was tempted—by the appearance of good.

Many Christians have expressed this exact concern about the *Twilight* saga: that Edward and the other vampires are precise examples of how Satan executes his most damaging attacks. It is in the beauty, the overwhelming appearance of perfection, that we mere mortals are easily lured into believing. Do you love *Twilight* because Edward is a beautiful temptation? We are drawn to beauty, as Christ is beautiful. But much of the time we don't exercise enough spiritual awareness to judge whether the beauty we see is real or an illusion.

An obvious example can be found on the cover of any glossy fashion magazine. The next time you see a picture of some starlet out running errands in a sexy outfit and full war paint, consider the stylist and publicist who just put a ton of billable hours into dropping "anonymous" tips to the local paparazzi and into getting her ready to leave the house. Then, of course, there are the pictures of models and actors that have been Photoshopped, stretched, airbrushed and tweaked to an unrealistic perfection. These photographs are fiction— just as beautiful and benevolent vampires are fiction.

All that glitters is not gold. Christianity is not a mindless activity. 1 Thessalonians 5:21-22 makes it clear we are to be fully engaged in our world. "Test everything. Keep the good stuff. Stay away from every kind of evil." The great news is that we are not defenseless. Not only is Satan a toothless lion; we are suited up to serve in the army of our victorious king.

Ephesians 6:10-18 gives us all the armor we need to be champion gladiators against evil. We are to wear truth around the waist, a breastplate of God's righteousness, sandals made from God's peace, a shield of faith that will stop any flaming arrow Satan may let fly, a helmet made of salvation and the sword of the Spirit, which is the word of God. We are decked out, and we are surrounded by millions of others just like us, fighting on the same team and fighting for goodness.

Remember: every good and perfect thing comes from God, but our enemy is a master of misleading images. Use your head. Ask questions. Praying all kinds of prayers and requests should always include this simple question: "God, is this a good thing/person/activity for me?" Listen for the answer. We are complete beings: body, spirit and mind. God intended for us to use every part of ourselves to discern good from evil, and find and follow goodness and trust.

The final word is the cross. It is empty. The grave is also empty. It could not hold our savior, Jesus Christ. He triumphed over death through his resurrection and life. 1 Corinthians 15:55 shouts, "O death, where is thy sting? O grave, where is thy victory?" Goodness and truth ultimately win. Our gracious God of love is more powerful than any evil.

To close, I offer a few quotes from the flyleaf of *The Screwtape Letters* by C.S. Lewis:

> The best way to drive out the devil, if he will not yield to texts of Scripture, is to jeer and flout him, for he cannot bear scorn.
> —*Martin Luther*

> The devil … the proude spirite … cannot endure to be mocked.
> —*Thomas More*

Chapter Worksheet

Suggested Group Activity

Gather several copies of newspapers and news magazines—enough for one per person or one per two people. Ask group members to find an example of evil or injustice at work in our world. They will need to summarize the situation they chose in a couple of brief sentences.

Put one chair in the middle of the group. Take turns sitting in the chair and telling about what was chosen and why. As a group, lay hands on the person sitting in the chair (his or her back, arms, hands, head) and have two or three group members offer prayers for the situation that was lifted up as an example of injustice or evil. End your prayers with the statements: "God is good. All the time. All the time. God is good."

Questions for Discussion

- What is your understanding of Satan?

- Have you ever heard the excuse, "The devil made me do it?" Do we have a choice, or are we controlled by powers beyond us? Explain your thoughts.

- Offer examples of what happens when a particular group or race or religion is vilified as evil by another.

- What is your understanding of the death and resurrection of Jesus Christ?

- What are ways we, as individuals and communities, stand against injustice and evil?

- What are ways we, as individuals and communities, work for peace and justice?

CHAPTER 12

To be Dazzling

THERE IS ONLY ONE thing Bella consistently asks of Edward: to be changed from a human into a vampire. Her motives change, depending on the conversation. She offers many reasons: to be less breakable, to be an equal with Edward in every way and, especially, to not be a temptation and hardship for him because of the blood in her body.

In the final book in the series, *Breaking Dawn*, Bella finally reaches a point where she is satisfied remaining human for a few more years. She and Edward get married and embark on a glorious, romantic honeymoon. Then the unthinkable happens: Bella gets pregnant. The half-human/half-vampire child grows at a phenomenal rate and acquires vampire strength even before birth. The child consumes all of Bella's strength while in the womb, even snapping her spine during birth. Only Edward's quick thinking saves Bella's life and, at long last, he changes her into a vampire.

As the transformation works its way through her body, Bella has time to think. The process is more painful than anything she has ever experienced: the venom burns through her veins as it changes her fragile human body into living stone. At first, while the fire rages through her, all she wants is to escape. Yet after a while, she remembers the reasons to endure.

Have you ever found the experience of being transformed by Christ to be painful?

Without knowing me—or that someday I would be writing about her books—Stephenie Meyer captured pretty closely the trajectory of my Christian walk. For decades after my salvation experience, I begged God for that secondary experience I'd been told was out there. I longed for sanctification so I would be "safe" from those constant dangers of sin and temptation all around me, much as Bella desired to be safe from the Volturi and other natural disasters through transformation into a vampire.

And, like Bella, I had no idea what I was asking for.

Very simply, there are three phases of spiritual life that my pastor explains through a sketch of three circles:

Circle of Rebellion   Circle of Debate   Circle of Full Surrender

The Circle of Rebellion is our natural state from birth. We spend all our time and energy running our own lives as we see fit, without even acknowledging God. This is symbolized by "Me" on the throne and the crown, or God, being outside the circle. John Wesley, the founder of the Wesleyan movement, referred to this period of time as the work of *prevenient grace*. *Prevenient grace* literally means to "come before" and is with us from birth: it recognizes the spark of divine light in each person, waiting to be set afire through the grace of God. Wesley described this grace as "free in all for all." *Prevenient grace* prepares the way for us to accept and experience justifying grace.

The second circle, the Circle of Debate, is where far too many Christians spend their lives. In the Circle of Debate, the individual is a believer and has asked God to come into his or her life through faith. She has acknowledged the sacrifice provided for her through Jesus. However, that person is still very much trying to run things as he or she sees fit. God is in this person's life, but not central—He is not given free rein to operate in full power.

Various faith traditions refer to the "Circle of Debate" experience of God's justifying grace using different expressions. Some identify this work of grace as *being saved, being born again* or *conversion*; Wesley described his experience as feeling his "heart strangely warmed." A person experiences justifying grace when he or she chooses to enter into a new life in Christ. Wesley would say that not only is grace "free in all for all," but also that we have free will and, therefore, a choice to make. We choose to accept or reject the free grace of God.

This is an experience of justification. One of my pastors used to say, "Justification means it is 'just as if' I had never sinned." The believer knows the power of forgiveness and enters into life in Christ.

The third circle, the Circle of Full Surrender, should be the ultimate goal of every believer. It is the point in time when the believer gives everything—*everything*—to God. It is when you step down, off the throne of self-determination, and yield completely to God.

There are nearly as many terms describing this third event as there are denominations. Growing up, I heard *sanctification* and sometimes *second work of grace* as something to aspire to and pray for. Until I saw the diagram, I had a hard time really getting a handle on this experience. This is the grace that moves the believer to "go on to perfection." Wesley referred to *justifying grace* as "choosing to open the door of God's house and entering inside." *Sanctifying grace* was "making God's house your home."

Using *Twilight* as an analogy: At the time Bella moves to Forks, she is in the Cullen equivalent of the Circle of Rebellion; or, perhaps we can call it the Circle of Ignorance. Although Bella had a feeling that she was different and destined for something, she didn't know what. Nevertheless, from the time she meets Edward until they decide to be a couple, Bella is in the first circle, refusing to really let him into her life. This is where we are before we meet Jesus and ask Him to come into our lives.

After Bella and Edward agree that they are in love with each other, Bella is in the Circle of Debate. Think about how much time she spends pestering Edward to be changed into a vampire; and think about how much she has to go through until that happens. The Cullens—Edward, Alice and Rosalie especially—insist Bella have "human" experiences while she can, because after the change, they will not have the same impact.

For me—although I was saved and Jesus was an important part of my identity and life—I had to get over "human" experiences that had influenced me before I could fully surrender into the third circle.

You see, while I grew up very safe and sheltered in an unbroken family and immersed in church, I had issues. I was the good kid. I was the one who memorized the most scriptures. I sang church solos. Yet my pride was strangely twisted with cripplingly low self-esteem. I had somehow confused humility with letting others win. I never saw anything beautiful in myself. I didn't want to let anyone see that I was smart, so they wouldn't think I was vain. I never wanted anyone to know how much all of that hurt me.

Years ago, before modern treatments made healing from burns less painful, the only way to heal from a massive burn without disfiguring scars was to continuously pull off the scab. If the scab was allowed to stay in place, the skin underneath would be puckered and crisscrossed with lines. However, if the scab was pulled off—a traumatic and painful experience of its own—fresh, smooth skin would grow. I was a mass of scar tissue. God had to peel off each of those "I-scabs" so that complete healing from bad teachers, misunderstood lessons and the natural results of willful disobedience could be cleaned up and replaced with a new, fresh heart.

Can you guess where I'm going with this? Can you see why I chose the scene from *Breaking Dawn* where Bella *finally* gets the one thing she wanted since deciding she wanted to be with Edward forever? The one experience of such great, unexpected pain that she later wishes she could simply die rather than finish out the transformation? Here's a hint…

> I beseech you therefore, brethren, by the mercies of God, that ye present your bodies a living sacrifice, holy, acceptable unto God, [which is] your reasonable service. And be not conformed to this world: but be ye transformed by the renewing of your mind, that ye may prove what [is] that good, and acceptable, and perfect, will of God.
>
> —*Romans 12:1-2*

A sacrifice is placed on an altar and burned. It is consecrated to God, made holy through its destruction. But we are living sacrifices: we have the option of crawling off the altar again. We aren't dead meat without a choice in the matter. We are corrupted from birth by our very nature, and things that have been growing inside all our lives aren't removed easily. We must be mindful of the purpose of our pain. There are things we have to let go of to become who God designed us to be. Remember that ripping off the scab and facing the cause of the original injury is necessary for complete healing—just like Bella, when she remembers there is a reason to endure the pain.

Jesus, in Paul's conversion experience on the road to Damascus, describes the process of sanctification as he lays out Paul's new career path in Acts 26:17-18. Jesus said (in paraphrase):

> Look, I am rescuing you for a purpose. Your calling is to open the eyes of the Jews and the non-Jews and to point them toward the light so they can see the difference between God and

Satan. Then they will be capable of receiving forgiveness and living lives that prove they have been changed.

Unlike salvation, that "eye opening," moment-in-time decision to invite Christ into your life, *sanctification*, is a process with increasingly evident results. It is a constant turning from darkness to light, of allowing the rays of Christ's love to penetrate the darkest corners of your heart and mind. It is rejecting the power of evil and accepting the life-giving influence of God through the Bible, good teaching and prayer. It is receiving forgiveness. It is coming to the place of realization that God loves you just as you are. It is as if God says, "You are good enough. Live this awesome life. And, by the way, you can forgive yourself as well!"

Paul's (a.k.a. Saul's) story in Acts 26 is one of the most dramatic in history. His adult life up to this point was all about defeating this new group of people that believed Jesus was the literal Son of God. The One Who rose from the dead and still lives, even after a gory Roman crucifixion. Paul was not above sentencing people to prison for their beliefs. And yet Jesus asked him in a flash of blinding light: "Saul, Saul, why do you persecute me?"

Now, this is a loaded question; the ultimate gut check. Paul believed he was doing God's business as a true and enthusiastic Jew. To have God question his motives turned everything on its head. (Paul knew instantaneously that this encounter was divine.) At that moment, Paul had to decide whether to cling to everything he'd ever been taught and perhaps lose the titles, respect and authority he held, or to serve this Jesus—the One Whose story he'd been trying to eradicate all along.

In making that choice, Paul experienced what he pronounced, years later, in his letter to believers in Thessalonica:

And the very God of peace sanctify you wholly; and [I pray God] your whole spirit and soul and body be preserved blameless unto the coming of our Lord Jesus Christ. Faithful [is] he that calleth you, who also will do [it].

—*1 Thessalonians 5:28*

What I have learned, and what Paul testified to, is that we cannot wish ourselves into the third circle—just as no amount of begging and wheedling on Bella's part would sway Edward. Our transformation is through divine timing and divine grace as we walk forward into God's word and will. It took time to accumulate a lifetime of scars, and it will take time to heal them. But "circle three life" is available to you.

Sanctifying grace comes not through good works or pulling ourselves up by our own bootstraps; it comes through God's transforming work in our hearts, minds and souls. Open your heart and allow the grace of God to mold you into a new person in Christ. Through this experience you will receive abundant life, full and overflowing. Paul, who knew what he was talking about, assures us that "the One who calls you is faithful and will do it."

Chapter Worksheet

Suggested Group Activity

For most people, there is a decision or an experience of accepting God's gift of grace. Some say it was a gradual awareness or realization that grew and grew; others point to a specific date and time. Wesley described it as feeling his "heart strangely warmed." Begin by making a list of common phrases used to describe this transforming experience. Next, ask the group to think creatively, using different words to describe this experience. Give group members time to think about it. It might be helpful for them to write down their ideas first, before sharing thoughts with the group.

Going Deeper
Bible Study

Have you ever felt you've somehow been confined to the shallow end of the Christian Life Pool? That what you've experienced so far can't possibly be all there is?

- In Romans 12:1-2, Paul addresses his fellow believers and calls them to a deeper life.

- At what point in history did a "second outpouring of grace" become a part of the Christian vocabulary? (Read Acts 1:1-5, and Acts 2:1-18.)

- What did the disciples have to go through to get to this point?

- Read Matthew 4:18-22.

- Skim Matthew 5-7; see any pattern in the sub-headings? So, then, what were the disciples doing?

- Skim Matthew 8-9, and ask the same questions.

- What happens in Matthew 10?

- What spiritual lessons did the disciples learn in Matthew 26:47-56?

- Matthew 27:45-61?

- John 20:1-9, 19-31?

- How necessary, do you think, were the two years between accepting the call to follow Jesus and the "second baptism?" Why?

- Where do you stand in the aforementioned growth process?

- Is there anything you can do to move yourself toward the experience of sanctifying grace?

Questions for Group Discussion

- How familiar are you with the concept of three phases of spiritual growth?

- How would you interpret your personal stages of commitment, or awareness of God's grace, in your life? Can you name other illustrations or examples that help you?

- What expectations do you have of yourself and of God at each of these stages?

- How can you be a *means of grace* for someone struggling with faith questions?

CHAPTER 13

A Very Talented Family

THE VAMPIRES OF THE *Twilight* saga are spectacularly beautiful, phenomenally fast and insanely intelligent. They also have special talents—abilities above and beyond what they already have. For example, Edward can hear the thoughts of anyone near him, except for Bella's. Alice can see snippets of the future as it pertains to her friends and family. Jasper can excite or calm the moods of the people around him.

After Bella is transformed into a vampire, she finds herself disappointed not to have a special gift. Then, a friend of the family points out that Bella still keeps her thoughts to herself—she is immune to vampire talents that attempt to control or read her mind. Bella is a shield. When it comes to the epic battle of good vs. evil at the end of the final book, it is Bella's shield extended over her friends and family that saves the day.

The church I grew up in was of the more conservative sort. We sat serenely through the sermons. Occasionally one of my great-aunts would give a hearty "Amen!" to a sermon point. Nobody ever ran in the aisles or danced for joy. Heaven forbid someone would stand up, uninvited, during the sermon to say a little something himself. The service ended promptly, and on time. We expected to be out by noon.

I'd heard of Pentecostals who did theatrical things. In fact, I knew a few, and they were very nice people. However, that kind of spiritual enthusiasm was looked upon with suspicion in my church. We preferred and cultivated the "quieter" gifts of the Spirit. We especially liked the gift of silent prayer. The gift of faith was also very popular. A few people were even very wise. In hindsight, though, there seemed to be a lack of vitality that would have brought even those quiet gifts to life.

Perhaps you don't know what I mean when I talk about "gifts" in this way.

Did you think the Father of Light would leave you without defense or resources for this lifelong journey? Oh, no. God's got it all worked out in an amazing way. If you think that what Jasper or Alice does is amazing, wait until you see what talents God has in store for you!

Look up 1 Corinthians 12:4-11. The first thing to note is that, although gifts vary, their purpose is the same: to support and grow the Church, reaching out to unbelievers and bringing them into a place of healing and growth. Here is a breakdown of the gifts noted in Corinthians:

- Message of Wisdom: The ability to speak well and wisely.

- Message of Knowledge: Like the Message of Wisdom but more specific to religion, like preaching and teaching the Bible.
- Faith: Trust in the presence and nature of God.
- Healing: Having the means to cure the body and soul of illness.
- Working of Miracles: The ability to cause the miraculous to happen.
- Prophesy: Divinely inspired speech declaring the purposes of God. Such speaking may indicate future events, call out the wicked or comfort people who are suffering. The Book of Isaiah is an example of all three in one.
- Distinguishing Between Spirits: Also called discernment, it is the ability to know if someone is on the level, or if their intentions are not as they seem.
- Speaking in Tongues: The ability to speak in different languages.
- Interpretation of Tongues: Interpreting languages.

Can you see the link I saw between the Cullen clan and these few verses? Isn't Alice the personification of prophecy and Carlisle, of healing? In *Breaking Dawn*, other immortals demonstrate additional gifts, such as Siobhan's faith and Eleazar's discernment.

At the end of this chapter is a chart that breaks down the gifts in 1 Corinthians 12:7-11 by their definitions and applications.

This is a difficult topic to discuss in our modern empirical age. We have been trained that if it can't be smelled, seen, tasted, quantified and documented, than it's simply not true. But things of the Spirit are not measured in quantifiable terms. God cannot be fully explained. If we could completely comprehend and define God, it would not be God. God is greater than that. God is perfect love and perfect truth. God is also mysterious and glorious. The ways of God are not the ways of humankind. God does not fit into a neat, tidy box. In the same way, the gifts of the Spirit are also "outside the box."

We have been trained that if it can't be smelled, seen, tasted, quantified or documented, then it's simply not true. But things of the Spirit are not measured in quantifiable terms.

There is a huge hunger in humankind for the spiritual. This hunger seems almost instinctual. There is barely a night when one won't find a television show being broadcast about ghosts, spirits or hauntings. Even the History Channel spends almost as much time on prophesy as it does on the past. Perhaps that is why I felt I'd finally come home when I "stumbled," by divine appointment, onto a very Pentecostal Bible study at a very trying time in my life.

In this group, I witnessed prophesy, speaking in tongues, translating, praying in tongues and all sort of other gifts my conservative denomination held at an arm's distance. But this group didn't care where I came from; its members welcomed me with open arms and nurtured me until I was spiritually healthy.

Warren, the leader, was a little troll of a man. Like Isaiah 53:2: "… he had no beauty or majesty to attract us to him, nothing in his appearance that we should desire him." Yet within weeks he was more precious to me than any other, more handsome preacher I'd ever met. Warren taught God's word with an insight and honesty I'd never experienced before. He was not afraid to display the most shameful and embarrassing aspects of his past if it helped clarify Scripture or illustrate God's grace.

It was Warren's gift of discernment that revealed my burden of low self-esteem; what's more, he showed me how to cast it off. My new friends, praying over me in tongues, prepared me to leave the corporate work world and enter youth ministry. It was during those cherished gatherings of honest people that I found a safe place to examine my motives and to replace them with God's. It was there that I began to walk and work in the gifts God had placed within me: faith, prophecy and knowledge. The result of the application of those gifts is this book, now in your hands.

I also know this: without the mentoring and teaching of that special group, those wonderful spiritual gifts would still be carefully wrapped and sitting on a shelf in my heart— unopened, unused and grieved as wasted by God, Who picked them out especially for me. Those group members were *Twilight*'s Kate and Zafrina to me, patiently correcting my mistakes and encouraging my practice until I was strong enough to work them on my own and, now, to teach them to you.

But as much as I would like, I cannot mentor all of you. You must find your own church, your own faith community and your own eternal family, where you are safe and encouraged to practice your spiritual gifts for the benefit of the Kingdom of God.

Each person is endowed, by the Creator God, with gifts. We each have things to offer for the building up of the Kingdom of God and the community of faith. The gifts differ. I have presented for you the gifts described in Corinthians for the early body of believers. The church or community of faith should still be a place where people not only discover their gifts but also practice, cultivate and mature in the use of their gifts.

Wisdom	Ability to give good advice, the best for each situation—frequently much different than what a non-Christian would give.
Knowledge	Moral insight relating to Christian life—it is the application of Biblical wisdom to a given situation.
Faith	A lasting, unshakable conviction in God and your relationship to him.
Healing	Both miraculous healing and medical skills are included.
Miraculous Powers	For miracles outside of physical healing.
Prophecy	Teaching Christ to come and the Christian life, the ability to understand and explain obscure parts of scripture, as well as divinely granted insight into the future.
Distinguishing Between Spirits	Ability to know if someone's intentions are honorable. Able to recognize instantly the Spirit of Christ in a fellow believer.

Speaking in Different Tongues	Literally in other languages without education. Often understood as a "prayer language" to communicate soul to God without self-censoring (see 1 Corinthians 14:1-5), also a means of communication from God—when used with the gift of interpretation.
Interpretation of Tongues	To translate and clarify a public speech in tongues for encouragement or prophetic purposes (see 1 Corinthians 14:1-5).

Chapter Worksheet

Suggested Group Activity

Prepare a handout with each group member's name listed. If possible, give each person a small gift box or gift bag. Distribute copies of the handout. Beside each name, direct participants to write the gifts they appreciate or can identify in that person. Ask: "What qualities or gifts do you see in this person, or what has he or she offered for the edification of this group?" These gifts might not necessarily be those listed in Corinthians. Other gifts group members may have include the gift of hospitality, acceptance, compassion, forgiveness or encouragement ... the list goes on and on. Tear or cut apart the papers so each person can receive what has been written about him or her. Instruct each person to put the slips of paper into his or her gift box to take home and read.

Together, offer prayers of thanksgiving for the gifts given and practiced by group members.

Going Deeper
Bible Study

To recap: We've seen that we have a choice in this journey. We can choose a loving God Who longs to hold us safe and to give us the best possible life. This is the God Who calls us *beautiful* and truly means it. Once we've chosen to follow God, we begin to grow up. We gain self-control over sin and over our own selfish desires. We begin to understand the deep love that drove God to allow the sacrifice of His Son. We learn what to do when we feel Jesus is nowhere to be found.

We've learned about the enemies of the soul: empty threats and truly dangerous ploys. But we have armor to protect us, and now we have gifts. How cool is that?

Read 1 Corinthians 12:7-11. Of the gifts listed, which appeals to you most? Why?

Read 1 Corinthians 14:1-5. What are the benefits of speaking in tongues? Of prophesy?

Why do you think the gift of tongues has been so controversial or misunderstood?

Questions for Group Discussion

- Think of a person who has been a spiritual mentor or teacher to you. What special gifts contributed to this person's ability to nurture faith in you and in others?

- How do we help others discover their gifts?

- What behaviors/ beliefs thwart the development of spiritual gifts?

- Relate a time or experience when you discovered or became aware of one of your spiritual gifts.

CHAPTER 14

Part of Our Family Now

THE CULLENS, FOR THE most part, welcomed Bella with open arms—as a family member, that is, and not as a meal. The exceptions were two of Edward's siblings: Jasper, who was still working on self-control, and Rosalie.

In Bella's mind, Rosalie had it all. She was the most exquisitely beautiful member of the family and had found her perfect mate in Emmett. Yet Rosalie harbored an undisguised resentment toward Bella. This is evident in both the book, *Twilight,* and the movie. In one instance, Edward asks Rosalie to trade clothes with Bella so as to hide her scent from another clan of vampires intent on hunting and destroying her. Rosalie refuses. Carlisle, the father figure of the Cullen clan, speaks up and announces that Bella is family now—and will be protected with the same degree of effort as would be given to any other family member.

One of the hottest words in advertising is *clanning*. To "find your clan" is to find the place in the world where you fit. It is how the athlete finds a team; the politician finds a party; and a *Twilight* fan finds Team Edward. The point of *clanning*, according to trend watcher Faith Popcorn, is "looking for commonality without going outside of your cocoon."

This is not a new trend: only the technology facilitating a clan's ability to go global is unique to our era. Just 20 years ago, parents of second-graders *clanned* at PTO meetings. Now a Google search pulls up more than 14 million "parent of second-grader" sites in less than 1/10th of a second! But, like second grade, clans don't last forever. Over the past decade my clan has shifted as my life has changed: from journalists to youth pastors to stay-at-home moms to authors. My place of commonality has changed as I have needed to seek out new areas of expertise and support. My journalism colleagues were great people, but of limited help and support when I became a youth minister and had a spiritual growth question. Likewise, I didn't know any youth ministers who were also stay-at-home moms when that phase of my life rolled around. The end of each chapter of my life marked the end of each clan's usefulness to me. The possible exception is the group of moms. The depth of education and breadth of experience these women bring to my life is really impressive!

There is a clan, in the much older sense of the word, that doesn't move when we do: family. Family is the lifelong network of support that hopefully strives for your continued improvement, growth and well-being. Unlike other clans, family can take you outside your comfort zone. For a family to be healthy, the members must confront one another and be confronted for the sake of addressing behavior and attitudes. Family members protect one another and, in turn, are protected both from external and internal dangers.

In the *Twilight* series, a vampire clan has developed: the Cullens. The Cullens are a group of vampires who have chosen to live as family. In choosing this family and adhering to their code of conduct, the individual members find a greater chance for survival than if they lived alone.

I am aware that some people don't want to—or even shouldn't—hold their biological family that closely. Fortunately, God has provided a clan for us—one that doesn't leave when we change, but cheers as we grow and, in turn, grows with us. It is the Body of Christ, the Family of God. It's been said that good family members offer one another both sandpaper and blankets. They love us enough to hand us the sandpaper when we need to work on our rough spots, and also know when we just need the comfort of a warm blanket to keep safe and secure. That's the kind of clan I'd like at my back.

How do I know there is a place for everyone in God's family? I've read the promise myself.

> Sing unto God, sing praises to his name: extol
> him that ride(s) upon the heavens by his name
> (LORD), and rejoice before him.
> A father of the fatherless, and a judge of the
> widows, [is] God in his holy habitation.
> God set(s) the solitary in families: he bring(s)
> out those which are bound with chains: but the
> rebellious dwell in a dry [land].
> —*Psalms 68:4-6*

God sets the solitary in families. Not in clone groups—in families. You know, the kind with crazy uncles and aunts who talk too much and grandmas who pinch cheeks even though you're way too old for that kind of affection. God loves our individuality; we were made unique on purpose. To me, this is both immensely comforting and hugely irritating. I'm "on purpose?" Yay! That relative who makes me cringe? Not so much! And that's part of where the growth comes from. Among the most valuable and difficult lessons of family are tolerance and appreciation. Because, after all, while we are unique, God does not rate us by our talents, features or personality profile.

> For ye are all the children of God by faith in
> Christ Jesus. ... There is neither Jew nor Greek,
> there is neither (slave) nor free, there is nei-
> ther male nor female: for ye are all (the same) in
> Christ Jesus.
>
> —*Galatians 3:26,28*

In spite of our external differences, we are all united. In that same chapter in Galatians, Paul warns us not to be distracted by the appearance of our fellow Church members. It is all too easy to scorn the lack of fashion sense in or unruly children of our fellow family members, when we *should* be focused on being one in Christ and lifting up our family members in prayer and love. We need to see beyond what separates us and remember that we are all shining souls and equally precious to God.

Remember those spiritual gifts we talked about in the last chapter—the ones described in 1 Corinthians 12:1-11? Why has God given you amazing gifts if you are going to live in a vacuum or a clone colony, where everyone is just like you?

The answer to that is found in the rest of the chapter, 1 Corinthians 12:12-20. You weren't designed to live alone. You weren't designed to thrive apart from the Church, aka, the body of Christ, because you are a vital part of that body. You need the rest of the body to survive. Verses 15 and 16 are actually almost funny: a foot cannot decide to leave the body just because it would rather be a hand, neither can an ear just drop off and crawl away, offended, because it can't become an eye. And if a foot or an ear could leave in a snit, what would happen to the body left behind? It is now incomplete, crippled. Talk about a vivid picture of a dysfunctional family!

Like the various parts of our bodies so marvelously designed and amazingly irreplaceable, so are you to the Church. You have a skill set that makes you special to your family. In turn, the Church family has skills that will sustain and strengthen you.

Imagine you have been blessed with the awesome gift of performing miracles. That's a big, flashy gift that tends to draw attention! You would be wise to partner with someone who has the gift of discernment. By working together, you both use your gifts to bless those God has sent into your lives. Additionally, someone with the gift of prayer, above and beyond the prayer we are all called to participate in as we communicate with God, is another vital partner in a successful ministry.

Again, God does not rate his creations. Just as no sin is worse than another, no gift is more valuable or special than another.

When you go down that list of gifts and think in "family" terms, it becomes obvious that there are no spare parts. Each of us is unique and uniquely gifted. Each of us has a place of service or ministry within the body of Christ—no excuses or exceptions.

This kind of cooperation is impossible to achieve with our own power. An arm can point the way, an eye can see the direction, a foot (or two) can walk on the path, but no one has a gift that keeps everyone moving together. Instead we must rely on Christ, Who is the body's head, as described in Ephesians 4:15-16. Under Christ, the whole body, each church and each individual within the Church is held together and made useful.

It is an apt illustration. Without Christ's leadership we, like an amputated limb, are really worse than useless—dead and quickly rotting. The choice is crazy clear: live, thrive and find usefulness as a member of the body of Christ or not. Not live, not thrive, not find usefulness.

Yeah, I like useful too. So, welcome to the family!

Chapter Worksheet

Suggested Group Activity

Provide markers and paper. Each person is to think of all the "clan" groups he or she has been a part of in the past 10 years. (You can decide how many years to include in this, based on your group members' ages, etc.) For every clan group, have members draw a box. Inside the box, have them write words or phrases to identify and characterize the group or clan. Put a star beside any clan group they have been a part of for four years or more. Briefly have members share their pictures with one other person or, if you have time, the entire group.

Ask: What did you learn about yourself? What insight into your life did you gain from this activity?

Questions for Discussion

- What does *clanning* mean to you?

- What are the important functions of clans?

- What does your faith clan or faith community mean to you?

- How have you experienced God's grace through your faith clan?

- Describe ways your faith clan could be more open to those outside of the faith.

CHAPTER 15

Glitter in the Sun

BELLA HAD SEEN EDWARD in the sun before. If she had harbored any doubts about his identity, they were burned away by the light shattering off his skin like a million prisms.

In *New Moon*, Edward decides to take advantage of the shimmering aspect of his vampire nature to force the harsh hand of the vampire ruling class in Italy. It is halfway through *New Moon* when Edward believes Bella is dead, and he decides that if she is dead, he would rather be dead, too. By stepping out into the sun in a crowded city square of human tourists, the ruling vampire class would be forced to kill Edward for breaking the one cardinal rule of being a vampire: Don't get caught.

However, Bella isn't dead—and she does all she can to keep Edward from breaking that rule.

But what if *we* shimmered in the sun? What if we weren't supposed to keep it a secret?

Once, when I was about 19 and working in a fast-food restaurant, a co-worker asked me why I was so happy all the time. I stammered and shrugged and coughed out some sort of answer along the lines of, "I don't know." But I did know. My obviously visible happiness, that roll-with-the-punches sense of peace that kept me sane, was from Christ. Sadly, my fear kept me from sharing that glorious hope for the present and future with my friend, who was genuinely hungry for spiritual truth. He saw a difference in me so obvious that he was willing to risk embarrassment by asking a strange question. To my shame, I was afraid to answer his curiosity with truth.

Within seconds of that faithless comment, a verse I'd known since childhood came to mind:

> But in your hearts set apart Christ as Lord.
> Always be prepared to give an answer to every-
> one who asks you to give the reason for the hope
> that you have …
> *—1 Peter 3:15*

I found my co-worker a few minutes later and apologized for my cowardice. I told him I was a Christian and had a hope based on faith in Jesus Christ. He shrugged and said he pretty much figured that was how it was.

Becoming a Christian, by definition, means becoming Christ-like. You are changed in a deep and fundamental way, and it shows when you are subjected to the bright lights of life. Perhaps more metaphorically correct, your life glows against the darkness around you. Brace yourself, because you *will* stand out. We are called to be a light to the nations.

Which is how it should be. Actions always speak louder than words, and it is through our actions that we demonstrate our faith. We read in Scripture that faith without action is dead. Most of us are probably familiar with the Sunday School song that preaches, "This little light of mine, I'm gonna let it shine. Hide it under a bushel? NO!"

The Apostle Paul dealt with powerful Church leaders with low moral standards in Acts 22:30- 23:5. In this dramatic courtroom scene, Paul is on trial, accused of blaspheming God—high treason in Jewish theocracy, where the high priest stands in as king in place of God. Paul is a master of Jewish law and is defending himself, and his opening statement is a declaration of innocence.

Enraged, Ananias, the high priest, demands Paul be slapped in the face; basically passing judgment before the trial even started. Paul lashes back.

"May God slap you, you painted tomb! You claim to judge me with the law—but break the law yourself by having me slapped!?"

"Paul!" exclaim those standing near him, aghast at his outburst, "That's the high priest!"

To which Paul replied, "How could I have known that? If I had, I would not have offended him. For the law is clear: Do not slander your leader."

How did Paul make such an egregious error? Josephus was a historian who documented life in first century Israel. By birth he was Jewish royalty, by training a priest, by practice a soldier and by vocation a writer. What makes his observations interesting is that he wrote from a political and social point of view about the world Paul saw from a theological point of view. Josephus had a few words to say about High Priest Ananias, calling him profane, greedy and hot-tempered. Ananias had the clothing and social status of high priest, but internally he was anything *but* holy, which was readily apparent in his actions. Paul's remark emphasizes Ananias' less than priest-like behavior.

The biggest problem true glitter-in-the-sun Christians face is the disillusionment created by those who call themselves Christians but leave pain and destruction in their wake. Almost weekly, another priest is busted for pedophilia; another high-profile, charismatic pastor is arrested for soliciting prostitutes and/or skimming from the offering plates. These whitewashed walls, no more than mud bricks with a nice coat of paint, frequently stand in the way of anything we might say to convince our friends that Jesus is The Way.

St Francis of Assisi wasn't showing us a back door into ministry when he said, "Preach the gospel at all times and when necessary, use words." He was showing us how to truly make a difference through our day-to-day living. A lesser-quoted proverb attributed to the saint is, "It is no use walking anywhere to preach unless our walking is our preaching."

Who is the true follower of The Way?

In Luke Chapter 10, we read about a teacher of the law who questions Jesus. He asks, "What must I do to receive eternal life?" In other words, who is a true follower of God? Jesus, true to form, responds by asking another question: "What do you think?" The lawyer quotes the Shema, the rote answer: "You should love the Lord your God with all your heart, soul, strength and mind and your neighbor as yourself."

Of course that is the right answer, according to Jewish tradition. How often do we quote the correct Bible verse, smug that we have the right answer—the truth?

Jesus responds, "You're right, now go and do it." The intent of the Jewish lawyer is to test Jesus or push Him to say something controversial. So far, this hasn't worked, until he asks, "Who is my neighbor?"

Jesus next tells a story. Remember that stories are a great way to learn spiritual truths. This is common practice for rabbis. In all likelihood, this was an oft-repeated story. It begins: "A man traveled from Jerusalem to Jericho …" Here is my paraphrase:

So there was this Jewish dude traveling between the big cities. He was camel-jacked out in the middle of nowhere, stripped of everything worth anything, beaten and left for dead. Soon, a priest came through the same stretch of road. He slowed down when he saw the man lying there, but continued past as far on the other side of the road as he could safely go. He did not stop or offer any help.

Soon a Levite passed by. He also passed by on the far side of the road.

Everyone who heard the story Jesus was telling was nodding. Listeners knew the road: it was dangerous and steep, providing ample hiding places for thieves. They also knew the story. There would be three people who would come upon the wounded man and the third would be the hero. The third person would do the right thing. The third person would be the true neighbor. Yet just then, Jesus switched the characters and told a revised edition.

Finally, a Samaritan, traveling down the same stretch of road, stopped and helped the man. Not only did he offer compassion, but he loaded the man up on his own ride, walking beside his donkey the rest of the way. The Samaritan took him to a nice hotel and told the innkeeper to spare no expense taking care of the injured man, promising to reimburse any additional expenses when he returned.

A priest is, obviously, a priest—someone who you would expect to always do the right thing. A Levite is a member of the church staff. From landscaping to linens, these guys are saturated with church life. To give them both the greatest benefit of a doubt, let's assume they were heading up to Jerusalem for their turn to serve in the Temple and needed to be ceremonially clean to do that. Touching a dead person would jeopardize that function.

They forgot the message of Hosea 6:6: "I desired mercy, not sacrifice, and the knowledge of God more than burnt offerings." Certainly they'd known this passage since childhood.

Then along comes a Samaritan. Samaritans and Jews were like the Montagues and Capulets on a national scale. Certainly the injured man, numb and gasping for breath, didn't expect a Samaritan to help if his fellow countrymen and clergy wouldn't. But the Samaritan did. He acted mercifully. His mercy acknowledged God.

Jesus asked: "So of these three men, who acted neighborly to the robbery victim?"

The law expert who had posed the trick question had to answer honestly: "The one who had mercy on him." Notice that the lawyer could not bring himself to say "the Samaritan."

Jesus is blunt in His response. "Go, and be like that Samaritan." (Luke 10:30-37.) Jesus is saying that you should be a person who acts on your beliefs, and not just one who offers the right answers.

The Samaritan never said a word about his theology; he didn't need to. Can you feel the change of heart the listeners of this story must have had toward all Samaritans? In telling this story, Jesus makes it clear that help often comes from the least likely person. It is not enough to assume a role or identity if you are not true to your calling.

Christians are called to "glitter in the Son." By action and deed our faith is revealed. It should be as obvious as a vampire stepping out into the bright sunlight. The vampires' skin sparkles like diamonds, reflecting the light, according to the *Twilight* series. How does your life reflect the light of Christ?

> Then shall the righteous shine forth as the sun in
> the kingdom of their Father. (She) who has ears,

let (her) hear.
—*Matthew 13:43*

Chapter Worksheet

Suggested Group Activity

Pass out a small packet of glitter, a blank notecard and an envelope to each person. Ask group members to think about people they know and are close with who might need a word of faith or a word of encouragement this week. Provide time for them to write a note to that person. Tell them to put the glitter in a place at home or at work where it will remind them to "glitter in the Son" and reflect the light of God in their daily living. When everyone has finished, you may choose to say a prayer over the cards that the love and light of Christ will be shared through the offering of these notes.

(If you are feeling really wild and crazy, sprinkle glitter on the cards!

Or … the group could close by singing *This Little Light of Mine!*)

Questions for Group Discussion

- Why is it easy or difficult for you to talk about your faith?

- How do you live out your faith?

- Give an example of someone who lives a life of faith that inspires and encourages you. Think about what it is about that person that gives him or her the ability to reflect the light of Christ.

- How can we, as individuals and communities of faith, "glitter in the Son?"

CHAPTER 16

Forever and Forever and Forever

IN *BREAKING DAWN,* **BELLA** takes a moment to consider what it means to have become one of the immortal vampires. She realizes it is "the first and last day of forever" for her, and since she now has everything she has ever desired, she is fine with that.

Everyone has *forever* stamped upon her soul. And everyone gets to choose what his forever looks like.

In moments of irreverent bad taste, I joke that if I'm wrong about all this, and the best we can hope for is cosmic recycling, than I want to come back as a cat belonging to someone like me.

Think about it: unfettered access to a multi-level, climate controlled home; bright, wide window sills to sleep on; beds, couches and chairs at your disposal if the window sills aren't cutting it; someone to open and close doors at your bidding and an endless supply of crunchy cat food. In exchange, what is requested of you? Nothing!

Occasionally, my cats express gratitude by bringing me a dead mouse or mole. (I choose to assume it's not a thinly-veiled threat.) Cricket can be relied upon to grace my lap during my morning devotional time with his warm, constant, buzzing purr of praise.

So there you have it, my definition of Heaven: everything I could possibly need or want, with my gratitude expressed by gifts given out of my abundant blessings and regular fervent hymns of praise. (Ironically, when I think about it, this sounds an awful lot like my life right now. Maybe I should aim higher.)

In common usage, *Heaven* usually has two meanings. One: the ultimate best of something, as in, "ooooh, that dark chocolate mocha truffle is heaven!" Alternatively: the name of an actual place featuring a bunch of puffy, white clouds and people in unflattering tunics playing harps, with its gates guarded by some guy with a big, fat book.

How can one word come to symbolize both the best of something and a place that, in truth, could quickly become a personal ring of Dante's Inferno? Which is closer to the biblical truth? When you hear that the streets of Heaven are paved in gold, what does that mean? Do you picture streets *literally* paved in gold, or do you take this as a metaphor—that perhaps gold is so insignificant there that it is used to fill in the potholes?

I mean, really—harps on clouds? Oh, wait … there they are, in Revelations 15:2-3!

OK, so there's biblical precedent for harps, but clearly they're not for everyone—just those who fought a particular battle. And there is actually a book; a bunch of them, really.

> And I saw the dead, small and great, stand
> before God; and the books were opened: and
> another book was opened, which is [the book]
> of life: and the dead were judged out of those
> things which were written in the books, accord-
> ing to their works. … And whosoever was not
> found written in the book of life was cast into
> the lake of fire.
>
> —*Revelation 20:12, 15*

Please, please, pay close attention to these verses. "The dead were judged according to what they had done." Romans 3:10 makes it very clear. "As it is written, there is none righteous, no not one." You have not been good enough to earn your way into Heaven; no one ever has been or ever will be. It's simply not possible to get in on good behavior. Only redemption through faith in Christ—in a decision made to commit your life to Christ and to live as a Christian—will remove your records from the books of judgment and record your name in the Book of Life.

The One who reads the books and passes judgment is no one less than Christ Himself. I know with confidence that the "Jane Wells" pages of the other books are blank, except for the footnote that says: "Please refer to the Book of Life." If you're not sure about your recorded status, you may want to re-read chapter 1, as your place is yours to determine. Trust me on this one: the alternative is not at all attractive.

As for the clouds—according to Revelations, chapters 11 and 14, only Jesus and a few resurrected prophets get to ride on them.

So, now we have an idea of what Heaven is not. To define what Heaven is, we need to take a step back and define the Kingdom of Heaven. Remember when you first read the *Twilight* series and something inside you glowed, yearning for a world of perfect balance and immortal love? *That* is the divine spark, a faint ember of the Kingdom of Heaven, planted inside all of us since creation. It is God's creative signature and calling card. It is our immortal soul's yearning for the Immortal's eternal love.

The realization of that love and salvation brings about the Kingdom of Heaven on earth, as seen in our internal peace and motivation to do God's will. But that, in God's eyes, is merely the means to an end. His end game is to secure your safety and your company for eternity. But if it's not to sit on clouds and sing along with harps, then what's the point?

There is much speculation over the Book of Revelation. We know it was written by John on the isle of Patmos, and that it describes a dream or vision. John was exiled to Patmos by the emperor Domitian for preaching in Ephesus that Jesus is Lord and God; Domitian favored that title for himself.

There are numerous interpretations of this apocalyptic book. Revelations presents two worlds: the sinful world (referred to as Babylon the Great in Rev. 18:2) and a new world, or Holy City of God, or the New Jerusalem (Rev. 21:2). Some take these words quite literally and others seek the truths for living in Revelations. The interpretations of Revelations and Heaven are as diverse as hit TV shows, like *Touched By an Angel,* and as big as front-page news when dozens of families gave up their jobs and drove end-of-the-world campers across America in the summer of 2011.

Here's my take on it: In Revelation 20, after Satan has been defeated and thrown into the Abyss, Christ begins His 1,000-year reign over the earth. This is still the physical earth, and somehow people will have survived a dark and terrible time without consciously choosing Satan—but without choosing Christ, either. During that millennial reign, Christians who have lost their lives because of their faith will return with Christ.

That remnant of uncommitted will have an unprecedented chance to walk and talk with Christ in a world without satanic influence. What a remarkable point in history that will be!

After that time, the books of judgment and the Book of Life will be opened; the Final Judgment will occur, the unrepentant punished and the saved rewarded with eternal glory. The city itself—the New Jerusalem, as described in Revelations 21—is astonishing. Massive walls of gold, priceless jewels and the purest light will flood it all, for it will be the glory of God. Flowing through the city will be a river of the water of life, and on each side of the river stands a tree of life. (It's not clear if there are two trees or one, though I quite like the second image.) Most interestingly, though, is that while all who are there have achieved Heaven, the work is not done.

Well, *work* might not be the right word. How much work is it to say "thank you" for something you are really, truly grateful for? While here on earth it is so hard to see everything God is and everything He does for us. Our human eyes cannot see the thread He runs through every aspect of our lives, guiding us, providing better choices, and creating seen and unseen miracles. In Heaven, though, we will see clearly: we will know the depth of the debt he paid for our sins and our gratitude will flow over. Like my happy cat, we will be perfectly (purrfectly) content singing His praises forever. It's crazy to think about, but it will never grow old. It's not like we'll need to change gears to study for a math test, or get off the couch to make dinner, or quit whatever it is we're doing to do something else unpleasant or burdensome. Even though Heaven is laid out much like earth—there is a city, within which there are walls, plants, trees and water—there is no more pain. No more curse. No more tears. That thought alone will bring about a new round of praise!

Pause for a moment and remember the best moments of your life. Were you with people you loved? Were you somehow helping someone who needed you? Are there moments when you know you made a difference and it made you feel good? Most often, we'll find our best moments are when we're using God's gifts to us for His glory. Heaven is the place where all those golden moments of our lives are connected to their source, stretched out and magnified forever. It's a perfection that not even Bella can imagine! Perhaps that is why we are to spend so much time developing our spiritual gifts here on earth: because those skills go with us.

> Let not your heart be troubled: ye believe in
> God, believe also in me. In my Father's house
> are many mansions: if [it were] not [so], I would
> have told you. I go to prepare a place for you.
> And if I go and prepare a place for you, I will
> come again, and receive you unto myself; that
> where I am, [there] ye may be also.
>
> —*John 14:1-3*

How cool is that? The God Who designed the universe, from the ladybug's perfect adorableness to the eagle's majestic flight, is designing a room just for you and just for me. I'm quite sure I'll be singing, "Thank you, thank you, thank you!" to God for a very long time for yet another completely perfect gift. When Bella comments that it is the first and last day of forever, that is also what life in Christ is.

Eternity doesn't begin when you die. It begins here and now. When we pray the Lord's Prayer, we pray, "Thy Kingdom come, on earth as it is in Heaven." We are reminding ourselves that God's plan for the Kingdom is on earth as well as in Heaven. We have Kingdom work to do, here and now; it is the first and last day of forever. Go out there and glitter in the Son of God.

Chapter Worksheet

Suggested Group Activity

A meaningful way to end a small group study is with an Affirmation Circle. This will take at least 3-5 minutes for every person in the group. It is helpful to softly play meditative music in the background. Form a circle with some chairs, with room for one in the center. Each member of the group takes a turn sitting in the middle. The rest of the group offers prayers for that person. Encourage the group to offer thanks for that person and requests for guidance and wisdom. It is a time of appreciation and consecration for one another to God. When everyone has had a turn in the center, you may choose to close with a common prayer or a scripture that you say together.

Questions for Group Discussion

Create for the group your vision of Heaven. (The author described it as coming back to life as her cat.) You could take time to draw pictures of Heaven and then share them with the group.

- How has literature and media contributed to our ideas and visions of Heaven?

- What does it mean to you if eternity begins in this life, and isn't just about the afterlife?

- What experiences have you had with death—and how did these experiences shape your faith and beliefs?

- What do you most hope for in Heaven? What is your greatest desire?

CHAPTER 17

About Small Groups

Why Small Groups?

Small group Bible studies provide unique opportunities for groups of 8-12 people, so that members can experience spiritual growth through discussion and encouragement. Small groups can help people process not only what they have read but also their own faith experiences. They provide group support for each of the members. Their effectiveness depends on each member's willingness to participate—to be authentic and to open his or her heart. Small group time is sacred time, if regarded as such. As the leader of a small group, you should be deliberate about facilitating interaction so that everyone has a chance to participate.

Where to Meet

Small groups work best in spaces that provide privacy for discussion. Groups have met in public parks, coffee shops, dorm rooms and living rooms. Find a time and place, with adequate parking and a degree of privacy, where people can easily gather. Some groups rotate their meeting place to accommodate different members.

The Agenda

If possible, provide a snack or a beverage while everyone is gathering; group members could take turns with this responsibility. Name tags are helpful when forming new groups.

Decide to either allow a brief time so that members can informally chat with one another or structure a check-in time. If folks are not well acquainted, it is helpful to go around the circle and ask each person about his or her week.

For check-in time, quickly go around your circle and ask each person to relate how he or she is doing. This will come easier the longer the group is together. During check-in there will not be discussion. Group members are to **listen** to one another, as members report how their week went, how they are feeling, what they are concerned about, etc.

An important aspect of a small group Bible study is sharing personal concerns and prayer. Begin your small group time in prayer. Invite members to hold hands and pray together. You could lead the prayer, or ask if someone would like to volunteer to pray. Honor both the prayer requests that have been voiced and those that remain silent. Ask that God impart wisdom, understanding and compassion onto the group. After the opening prayer, move into a discussion of the assigned chapter and work through the study questions found at the end of each chapter.

Group Discussion

You may want to begin by reading a quote from the chapter, or by asking someone to summarize the assigned chapter. Choose one of the questions to begin a discussion. You or the group can decide: if the question just isn't working for group members, move onto another question. It is not important to use all of the questions, but rather to find the ones that will be meaningful for your particular group.

Give **everyone** in the group an opportunity to speak. As a leader, be deliberate about drawing out the opinion of those who tend to not express themselves as easily as others. What's often most difficult is the responsibility of tactfully cutting off members who might monopolize the conversation.

Honor all members by keeping to the allocated time schedule. Close with a group prayer.

Attitude of Gratitude

Encourage open and honest discussion. If the group is judgmental or disapproving of conflicting opinions, this will not happen. As in any family, there are bound to be disagreements. Create a safe atmosphere. Ask members to be open-minded, accepting of differences and charitable to one another.

There is no such thing as a stupid question if the questioner is sincere in seeking the answer.

Group Responsibilities

Ask group members to lift one another in prayer throughout the week. Consider a rotating list of responsibilities, such providing snacks and drinks, preparing or scheduling the meeting place, sending meeting reminders and preparing group greeting cards for all to sign (get-well cards, celebration cards, etc.).

If the group really bonds, you may decide to continue discussions even once you finish this book. There are additional resources available for small groups. Of course, we suggest you first look at www.readthespirit.com for more resources for faith communities. There, you will find an eclectic variety of viewpoints, of faith traditions and of soul-searching resources for small group study.

CHAPTER 18

Breakout Study Options

IF YOUR GROUP CANNOT commit to 16 weeks on the same theme, here are some options for a shorter series:

Movie Clip Conversation Starters

Play the following movie clips and ask the corresponding questions to open the small group discussion. The questions below are designed to segue into the Bible study questions at the end of each chapter.

Chapter 1: *Twilight* Scene 1, 0:00-2:35

- What is the hardest choice you ever had to make?

- Was your choice between two things equally good or between two things equally bad?

- Were the consequences as good or bad as you expected?

Chapter 2: *Eclipse* Scene 3, 21:00-24:00

- What would change in your relationships if you loved or were loved like this?

- Have you ever considered that someone might be able to love you so completely and unselfishly?

- Does being secure in a relationship change the way someone interacts with the world? In what way?

Chapter 3: *Twilight* Scene 14, 107:15-110:15

- Do you ever have difficulty trusting people?

- Why?

- Which is harder to do: build trust or destroy it?

Chapter 7: *Eclipse* Scene 11, 110:50-113:00

- Why does Charlie assume that Bella and Edward are having sex?

- Is that a fair assumption?

Chapter 11: *Twilight* Scene 11, 52:45-54:00

- What is a temptation that almost always gets to you?

- Can you share with the group your best temptation resistance techniques?

- Is there something the same at the root of every temptation? Vanity, a sense of entitlement, pride?

Chapter 14: *Twilight* Scene 18, 129:30-131:15

- What sorts of surrogate family members do we surround ourselves with?

- What holds these family members together?

- What are the best and worst parts of being in a family?

Chapter 15: *Twilight* Scene 10, 49:35-52:30

- Why doesn't Edward ever go out in the sun?

- What would you think if you saw someone walk through a patch of sunlight and he or she suddenly burst into a reflective light?

- Think of a time when you stood out or felt different. Was it a good or a bad experience?

Breakout Options

Four-week Breakout: Who You Are

- Chapters 1, 2, 4 and 8

Four-week Breakout: What You Fight

- Chapters 5, 6, 7 and 11

Four-week Breakout: Spiritual Growth

- Chapters 3, 10, 12 and 13

Eight-week Breakout: Beginning to End

- Chapters 1, 2, 5, 8, 10, 12, 14 and 16

About the Author

There are only a few things Jane Wells loves more than reading fiction: God, her family and writing. When she's not vacuuming up after Golden Retrievers or picking up after her sons, Jane blogs about fiction, her life, and how they intersect at www.GlitterInTheSun.com.

Colophon

Read The Spirit Books produces its titles using innovative digital systems that serve the emerging wave of readers who want their books delivered in a wide range of formats—from traditional print to digital readers in many shapes and sizes. This book was produced using this entirely digital process that separates the core content of the book from details of final presentation, a process that increases the flexibility and accessibility of the book's text and images. At the same time, our system ensures a well-designed, easy-to-read experience on all reading platforms, built into the digital data file itself.

David Crumm Media has built a unique production workflow employing a number of XML (Extensible Markup Language) technologies. This workflow, allows us to create a single digital "book" data file that can be delivered quickly in all formats from traditionally bound print-on-paper to digital screens.

During production, we use Adobe InDesign®, <Oxygen/>® XML Editor and Microsoft Word® along with custom tools built in-house.

The print edition is set in Caslon and Gill Sans typefaces.

Cover art and Design by Rick Nease: www.RickNeaseArt.com.

Editing by Beth Miller.

Copy editing and XML styling by Stephanie Fenton.

Digital encoding and print layout by John Hile.

If you enjoyed this book, you may also enjoy

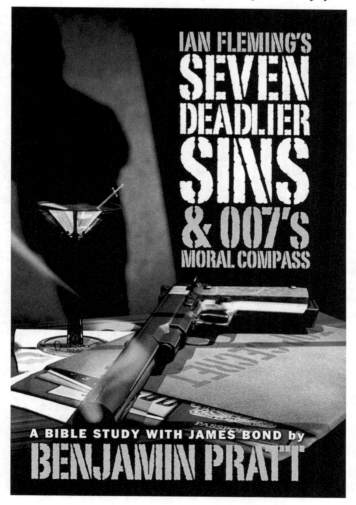

Here's a book that will reward your efforts as you look at evil through the eyes of Ian Fleming's James Bond. Like Bond, you too might be roused to take on the dragons of evil in our midst.

http://www.JamesBondBibleStudy.com

ISBN: 978-1-934879-11-5

If you enjoyed this book, you may also enjoy

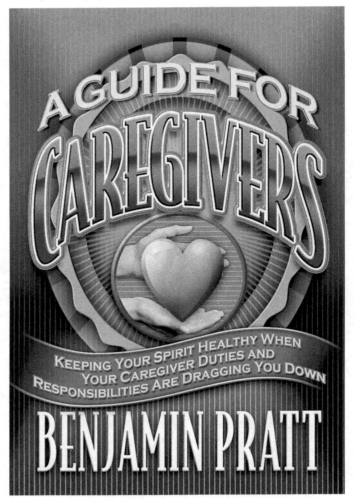

In one out of three households, someone is a caregiver: women and men who give of body, mind and soul to care for the well being of others. They need daily, practical help in reviving their spirits and avoiding burnout.

http://www.GuideForCaregivers.com

ISBN: 978-1-934879-27-6

If you enjoyed this book, you may also enjoy

Help in surviving the stages of grief and
bereavement after a loss

Guide for Grief

RODGER MURCHISON

In his new Guide for Grief, the Rev. Rodger
Murchison brings years of pastoral experience and
study, sharing recommendations from both scripture
and the latest research into loss and bereavement.
http://www.GuideForGrief.com
ISBN: 978-1-934879-31-3

If you enjoyed this book, you may also enjoy

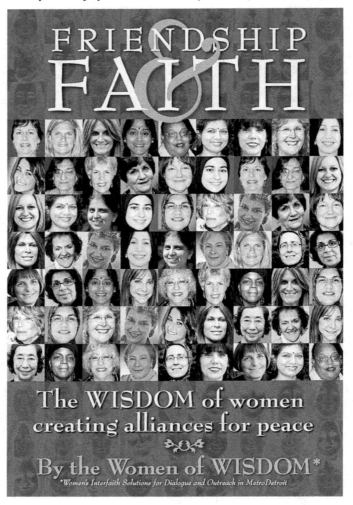

Finding a good friend is hard. Preserving a friendship
across religious and cultural boundaries—a challenge we
all face in our rapidly changing world—is even harder.
http://www.FriendshipAndFaith.com
ISBN: 978-1-934879-19-1

CPSIA information can be obtained
at www.ICGtesting.com
Printed in the USA
LVHW082154310319
612444LV00044BA/2347/P